"If there has not been such a thing as quantum poetics before, *Waling waling palpitations* cracks open the space for it. *These poems are multidimensional in the purest sense—multi-lingual, multimodal, multi-gender, multi-genre. They reach through time and space toward wounds ancestral and cultural, earthy and personal, then name them with an honesty as fierce as it is tender.* nawa is generous with images (both in lyric and visually) that stun and seduce as they navigate the impact of colonial exotification … 'my own trial is in not gentrifying myself,' and with those words, nawa opens the question of what true care means, for ourselves and our collective healing."
—**LISBETH WHITE**, AUTHOR OF *AMERICAN SYCAMORE*

"*Waling waling palpitations* is *a gallery, a performance piece, an assemblage, a field of flowers collaged with concrete and decolonization. angel's lyric prose and images create a dreamlike state where queer histories clipped before bloom are allowed to bud with possibility,* where orchids grow erotic rather than exotic and fiercely, devastatingly, Wild. *I left this work shaking with pleasure, my mouth full* of words sharp as bolos and soft as the silencing of the Waling-waling. If *Waling waling palpitations* is an altered state, let me never return to the norm."
—**JEN SORIANO**, AUTHOR OF *NERVOUS* & CO-EDITOR OF *CLOSER TO LIBERATION*

"A kaleidoscopic, multisensory, and mesmerizing work, *Waling waling palpitations* is a heart-wrenching spectacle, a fractal celebration of queer joy, a supernatural conjuration of matrilineal lineages past and present, a permutative drag performance, and *a true decolonial heartbreaking gesture that enters you, touches you, makes contact with every cell of your body and being, and carries you through an unbelievably beautiful and transformational journey.* 'i am what my mother hoped: something she could never know,' the text sings of impossible possibility. I have perhaps never experienced a book that I wanted to absorb into my own being so much. A work of unmeasured beauty and genius. You will be fucking changed by this book. Seriously."
—**JANICE LEE**, AUTHOR OF *SEPARATION ANXIETY*

"nawa angel a.h. is a writer who defies cultivators. Like the orchid, *Waling waling palpitations*, is intertextual in its form and is a queer plant species that has learned to survive a cultivator's hands. *The speaker tells the story of a closeted mother, an orchid who survived 'because she stifled herself from blooming,' and the queer descendants she produced who unfurl in your hands.* Call it epic poem, call it memoir, call it a colonial history, just know that as you read nawa angel a.h. is reading you too."

—**CORINNE MANNING**, AUTHOR OF *WE HAD NO RULES*

"Somewhere between performance, body, language, and image, there is an epic undulation that refuses to still. This book vibrated in my palms, recalling my body beyond reading. I always hope that books happen to me. This book blew open genre, gender, and biography, blooming like the waling-waling orchid into biomythology. An erotic song cycle. *A full-throated juice-laden hip thrust back at colonization. A primal skin scream. You cannot contain what you hold in your hands.*"

—**LIDIA YUKNAVITCH**, AUTHOR OF *READING THE WAVES* & *CHRONOLOGY OF WATER*

"To make this work a specimen is to find it rejecting the pin, slithering from the page of its definition. Instead, *engage as willing tribute, as response to the call, as witness and chorus, and find all your senses flung wide.*"

— **AMBER FLAME**, AUTHOR OF *APOCRIFA* & *ORDINARY CRUELTY*

"nawa alviar horton presents a wailing elegy of Diaspora through an intergenerational tale of the many orchids, vandas, and waling walings that persist across the projecting shadows of the US occupation of the Philippines. *Carrying us across their tongue like Gloria Anzaldúa, we learn through magical realism how language oppresses us, how language holds us, and how language mis/retranslates us and our loves.* If you need a material way to grasp Ilocana history beyond textbooks, look no further than this text. Wherever in the book you come to understand it, this history is a much clearer declaration against dictators and dying genders than you will find. And in the face of it, you too may 'want to believe that (queer) love can change us.'"

—**DR. MAR AZIZ**, ASSISTANT PROFESSOR OF BLACK STUDIES, COMPARATIVE ETHNIC STUDIES & GENDER STUDIES, UNIVERSITY OF WASHINGTON

"*A beautiful and transcendent upheaval* that expands the bodymind of its readers to sit with the wounds of colonization and the resilience of queer love. These pages carry you through a tender-hearted experience of beings who know what it feels like to be simultaneously exotified and unrecognized. This is the kind of book that touches and reaches into the parts of you that *go beyond the thinking brain and into the wisdom, knowledge and memories of the earth that is your body.* I'm so grateful for this chimerical creation."

—**CHE CHE LUNA**, ECOEROTIC ARTIST & CERTIFIED SEX EDUCATOR

"nawa angel a.h. weaves lineages, possibilities, horrors, and necessary medicines of their transdisciplinary transfiguration ... *A gift to every child of the sun born from island sand and saltwater tears, this is prayer on page on sultry surrender to the parts of us that wail and howl only to the moon. Their writing reminds us that we are portals, infinite and of multitudes.* Their composition requires our indefinite commitment to queering every hair follicle on our (brown) honey sweet skin. May every one who lays sweaty palm unto these pages find themselves celebrated, whole, and without lack."

—**SAMMAY PEÑAFLOR DIZON**, FILIPINX AMERICAN CHOREOGRAPHER & INTERDISCIPLINARY ARTIST

"*A choreographic proposal* harvested from a lifetime being flesh, heart, lungs, eyes and bones. nawa offers a blending of public and private realms, a memoir and cultural storytelling, personal mythology and a relatable journey of a contemporary body, with an air of recommendation and ritual. Their reveal of maternal lineage in poetic dynamics is a resonant soul searching. They offer it through blended languages, through pockets of understanding and a simmer of confusion. Again making a dance out something deeply familiar, the life-long task of familial reflection. *nawa is orchid, orchid is nawa, ancestor, mentor, the deepest internal yearnings, and layered folds, and the most external thoughts, skin, lashes, lust and dew.*"

—**TAJA WILL**, ARTIST, WRITER, EDUCATOR & HEALING JUSTICE PRACTITIONER

"*Waling waling palpitations* pulses with ancestral memory and queer futurity, bursting open the boundaries of genre, gender, and geography. *a.h. has composed a living altar that is part orchidarium, part spellwork, part love letter to what refuses erasure.* This is not just a book, but an invocation: lush with Pilipinx fragments, drag incantations, botanical hauntings, and the ache of matrilineal loss and becoming. ***Every page unfolds like the waling-waling itself—rare, radiant, and impossibly alive.*** Prepare to be unrooted, rewilded, and remembered."

—REESE FERNANDEZ

"*Moonyeka writes beyond the colonial wreckage of language and gender*, through numbers and an alphabetic reckoning that moves from 'ABRASIVE' to 'EXECUTED,' birthing a book where an orchid is both oracle and offering. I felt the tug of ancestral memory in these pages—the ache of migration, the intimacy of shame, the insistence of Tagalog and Ilocano to be unsmothered. *This book is deeply political in the way the body is political: stitched, desired, dislocated, and insistent on survival.* Waling waling palpitations is an act of reclamation. In the bile and bloom of our mother tongue, Moonyeka's writing is furious and sensual, feral and alive."

—T. DE LOS REYES, AUTHOR OF *AND YET HELD*

"*Waling waling palpitations* *stirs the soul and suggests an ocean of mysteries.* Each image blooms like coral reef in color and solitude, eliciting meaning that asks the question *where am i from and where am i going?* Seafoam on the brow. Here and then gone, but a film of remembrance reminds me i am here. *A world unto itself, each piece adds a new color, shape, sound to the tide washing across the body. A ritual.*"

—IMANI SIMS, CREATOR OF THE DECK OF NONE

FIRSTMATTERPRESS

Portland, Ore.

WALING WALING PALPITATIONS

WALING WALING PALPITATIONS

nawa angel a.h.

FIRSTMATTERPRESS
Portland, Ore.

First Edition

Published in the United States
by First Matter Press
Portland, Oregon

Paperback ISBN-13: 978-1-958600-10-8
Library of Congress Control Number: 2025945044

Editors: ash good & Charity E. Yoro
Contributing Editors: Lauren Paredes, Hailey Spencer & Emily Moon
In Cohort: Violeta Garza, Annemarie Eayrs & Claudia Saleeby Savage
Contributing Readers: Sonya Wohletz, Andra Vltavín,
Corinne Manning & Callum Angus

Cover: *Waling Waling Palpitations* (digital art)
Copyright © 2025 by Pearlyn Tan
pearlyn.net

Book design by ash good
ashgood.com

This project was made possible by Regional Arts and Culture,
The City of Portland's Office of Arts & Culture, Oregon Cultural
Trust, and Multnomah County Cultural Coalition.

for qt descendants

always &

always

always

a dear friend

movements

EXPOSURE BLOOMS

face the sun & shove the stalker all the way to the bottom of the hardy leaf. then, send back the one hundred men and eight women that have called me delirious. i believed the first twenty nine. when parched from disbelief, i chew, puncture, and slip on words.

A— *ayayatenka is ABRASIVE*

B— *BARBARIC BRAZEN BAKLA BULAKLAK BREASTFEEDS. BALISONG BUTTERFLIES, BAGUIO*

C— *Are you COMFORTABLE, CULTIVATOR? COLONIZER? COMMERCIAL? CUNT!*

D— *DORMANCY & DESPAIR lasts six to nine months per DENIAL*

E— *ENDEMIC EROTIC*

F— *FOREIGN FLOWER (bulaklak). Orchids do not require FERTILIZATION. King FELIPE. FOUR thousand Spanish words inFILTRATED,*

G— *GENETIC, GENES, GENOCIDE*

H— *HOW does*

I— *INDIGO look in ILOCOS?*

J— *JUNGLE, JUGLAR, JUNGULAR*

K— *KISSES, KILIG*

L— *the four LETTER word is actually five,*

M— *MAHAL. MOTHER is MONKEY is*

N— *NANAY is*

O— *ORIENTAL ORCHIDACAE ORCHIS [see: testicle]*

P— *PARADISE, doesn't have PAPERS, doesn't have PRONOUNS* he-/shes

Q — *QUEER as in*

R— *people of the RIVER, RECLAIM, REVOLUTIONS against*
S— *SAMPAGUITA, a SPANISH flower (est. 1942)*
T— *TRAITORS are shot in the back. TRAITORS are TAGALOG.*
    TOUCH me not. THEY -/ siya
U— *UGLY because darker, wider*
L— *Vanda - LIFE, LUZONICO*
V— *Life— Vida, VANDA sanderiana*
X— *and EXECUTED*

The 5 W's:
W— *Who*— is wildy on trees, close to the sea
W— *What*— is overhanging in waves
W— *Where*— an orphanage, military base, Germany, Miami, Florida,
    Lacey, Washington, Coast Salish Sea, Coral Sea, Red Sea, Baguio,
    Philippines, Province,
W— *When*— CULTIVATOR *was only twenty years older than*   *when*
    he died.
W— *Why*— *the three hundred year plus colonial project failed*
    and we are HOW.

i deny myself, myself more times than i could count to ten in inglés.
i promise to forget the alphabet spewed by the eight Marcos loving
women who cannot fathom being exposed to the pine stuck sun.

isa:one

SANDERIANA is known for being SOLITARY.[1]

<hr />

[1][even the footnote is SLUTTY and STRONGLY clawed, especially in the springtime]

dalawa:two

I am FERTILIZED by two-parted sounds.

(i) *More than woooorrrdddsss is all I ever needed you to show me, and you wooouldnnn'tt haaavee to saaaay that you love me, becaaauuuuuse IIIIIIII allllreeeaaadyyy knoooooow.*

(ii) at 12pm sunday mass the sound changes to *ssseeccreeettss* hushed whispers by hat wearing church ladies, we're all catholic, but behind the gaggle of geese-y women; behind those white gloves they'll pray for the sinner in me and pray to our father art thou in heaven to protect them.

the radio is tuned into two bifurcated eras—

1970s - inay aida stalks my college like an undead hen, ensuring i chek into class. i did. then ran to Rico.
2000s – voice mail, nanay to anak: *Hoy, why your not pinking uhp the pone? Makesureyougotoclass, ah! No galibanting ehcross town, TitaMarieThess said she see you sa palengke kissing an Orchid, bobo! You think that's kyute, ah? Tanga! Don't embarrass me in pront of de whole kommunity!*

—in both i realize, i was not a seed, but a pit.

tatlo:three

April—March *she's tawny yellow with fuzzy red brown*
January—February *his throat is cream white and glossy.*
June—July *my lips are raised and very dark purple.*

apat:four

the denny's waitress → the auto repairman → bank of america teller
play telephone in front of me. ring ring ring! askin' about my mouth
wide shut, husband say:

> Vanda is from overseas, she can't understand you.

[laughing] HAUHHAUHHAUHHAUHHAUHHAUHHAUHHAUHHAUHHAUH *inhale*
[against] my neck. i clench
my [teeth] smile [my]
dimpled [face] into [an] open house, [encore!]
nod like barrel man [pretends to be] funny [as if]

                              [i have no idea what] he just said.

                              O— OVERSEAS
                              P— PHILIP, my husband
                              P— PHILIPPINES, my country

lima:five

dormancy lasts five to nine months.
my dormancy is rest.

P— PROTEST.

anim:six

every rose has its thorn, every orchid has its cultivator.

pito:seven

a hung man who've only ever hung men
know too much
or too little of H-
HERMAPHRODITES have the characteristics

of all sexes. perfect
bears both stamens and pistils, long

      threading roots forced into narrowing feet, and
does the heart not look like a testicle?[1]

[1] *a left*   *ventricle that will not*   *rub off easily.*

walo:eight

i have mimicked every frown of disgust back at myself. it's made me
closer to the translucent pink tomato'd children, sticky with emotional
neglect. those babies boomed, smelling like spoiled milk.

S for Sepals
P for Petals
O for Open
I for Inherit
L for Lips
E for
D for Dreams

ttt   tttttttttttttt
 c   t
 ix   xx
e   co
t
t   e   t t
i   ,   t
c   t
x   t
e
t   ,   t
o i   t
 c   t
 ix   xx
o t   t t
t   e   t t
o   c   e-   t   t
i   i   t   t
x   x   t   t
e   o   not   native   t   t
t   t   t   t
o   i   but,,,, ,   t   t
x   c   t   t
e   x   -   t
t   o   t   t
i   t   ,   t   t
c   i   t   t
x   x   t   t
e   o   t   t
t   t   , t   t
o   i   t   t
i   c   t   t
x   x   t   t

foreign.

Figure 1. [a diagram of   's sex   ]

Figure 2. Houses both the male (anther) and female (stigma) parts of the flower

Figure 3. Houses   the ma   n

Figure 4. Houses   (stigma)

Figure 5. Houses   her

Figure 6.   both   (   ) and   (   )

Figure 7. H   i   s

Figure 8.

flower

Figure 9. H us   h

Figure 10.   s   h h male   h

Figure 11.   s   h h   female

Figure 12.   s   h h   h   (s iy   a)

never a wallflower, choreographic notes

R to L: Hibiscus L. Aries S. Moonyeka

1   begin fused to a wall,
2   recount the protest song
3   peel off Trader Joe's market price
4   unwield.

on the floor, start center.
come towards the ticket holders, orchid buyers
7/8   assume the position of yearning even though
you don't.

Hibiscus begins center.
3/4   *DON'T.*
Aries also
6/12 *PRESS.*
then Moonyeka.
US.

1   approach with less caution

3   non flowers
5   even if you create distance,
7   it does not rid your background noise denial:

&8   that you could go unnoticed.

pp

we do not have the perks of being a wallflower.
we do not make

S— see
E— extractions
N— notice, but do not
S— succumb to
E— erasure

move like you're already disappeared, but
do not disappear yourself.
crawl. unpluck the obsessive
wonder(ing).

out yourself.

ORCHIDS ROLL THEIR EYES

Heavy

Into the back of their

pistols

We stand grotesque

In one of the largest garden pools

We,

waxy wet rainforest

We   (who)

Produces an orange to orange

sun lip

FOUL

SPOTTED

LICKING EACHOTHERS' SCENTS

THIS SPECIES OCCURS

WITHOUT CALLOUS MISNAMING

Our,

Swollen cloud lips require fire toothed

Fangs

throats

We   do best mounted.

Oblonging for leather dense

IF GIVEN
CONSISTENTLY
UNIFORM

MOISTURE

We

appear half open

AND

EASY TO FORWARD
PROJECT INTO A

tongue

CRAMP OUR ROOTS
TOGETHER UNTIL

odor

We

We   elongate cinnamon

and wait for the

heavily

blotched

horn.

THIS SPECIES
OCCURS WITHOUT

CALLOUS MISNAMING

You ,

Red eyed with reward

Sharply spined disgust creeps into a

15 - 25 CM ERECTION

You ,

Persist long after

FERTILIZATION

Even when the

OVARY IS VISIBLY FORE
FINGERED FOR AGED IT
BECOMES INCREASINGLY
RARE FOR VIGOROUS
GROWTH TO RAPIDLY FORM
AFTER OVERINDULGENT
CULTIVATION

WE TRANS
PLANTED

The visitations happen at the outer halves of bars

Several small insects question you at the *yellow side lobes*

OURSELVES BEFORE YOU EVER COULD.

LICKING EACH OTHERS' SCENTS

I started out as a yaya in 1987. I was hired to watch over General Frank Robinson II's family in Germany, I arrived two years into their stay— wiping their children's diaper rashed asses. I caught myself, binky in hand, lost between the lines of greedy-grinned, chocolate smeared mouths and the brim of foaming German beer—all of us a slug of passion, oversalted.

Ilocano words stayed on like skin tags, frequenting as freckles. I rid of every duende song sound I could, rubbing it off with St. Ives Apricot Scrub to do the job. The actual job I had, I am grateful for. Most days I stare out the wash window, losing the children in the white of the baby powder, the white of the snow, and the white of powdered sugar on mickey mouse pancakes.

The General would often set me up with one of his friends, Phillip. I never got fluent enough in German, English and direct eye contact to understand the dynamic. That was until Phillip's fiance found him in sin, cheating on her. She looked like me, but prettier and more respectable. I'm a distraction. A puta.

Either way, I wasn't interested. I haven't ever kissed a white man before. I haven't kissed a man before. I haven't kissed before. I haven't kissed. I have no kiss. I have. I. I have. I have killed. I have killed before. I have killed my only love long before.

The family was stationed in Orlando a few years later. Minnie Mouse at Disney World curtsey'd next to the fruit stands with watermelon and jicama. They never had vinegar on the side, *ew*, the children would say, *why would you eat it like that!* My hands sugar'd with watermelon seed, until I sucked my fingers until my gluttony inversioned on itself. The love I starved sold sliced pregnant fruits in plastic bags with me. I was eleven; eight years old siya. The fruit skin peels at-will under my touch sopping crush. Siya sliced the papaya's belly open, gutting the descendants. We offered the seedlings to the grown and I suddenly dreamed of what our split open bellies could make, two million seeds inside single vanilla pods, our own babies.

But how?

I cut the ribbons to condom the fruits. Those quick-to-go-rancid, gutted bodies became easy-to-travel carry ons for the passengers' three hour jeepney rides. When we were done with our morning shift, the back of our hands brushed hard enough to dissolve into desaturated blooms, two forget-us-nots who'd live in opposing pine filled rainforests. A whiff of any ocean made me feel the closest I've ever been to her.

I was 19 when I had to offload my body. I left Siya without sound.

Phillip trailed behind the family I nannied for, conveniently? coincidentally? cunningly? stationed at the army base nearby. Being the yaya also meant fulfilling my role as Phillip's trinket to the military ball.

I wore a blackened eggplant evening gown, a hand-me-down of his used-to-be missus. Missus Pia Angelique Diaz had left Philip back in Germany two weeks after their star-spangled engagement announcement at the drunken gathering.
Pia died suddenly. Died of barbiturates. Died with a diamond ring, bigger than her prismatic puso. I slipped into the gifted dress. I carried on most like a longanisa—compact, wrapped raw, meaty and filled. My chest gaped at the top of the sweetheart neckline, the ghost of my breasts met the eeriness of the fabric's last ruffled memory of skin. I am not her. But we are touching now. her. the ex fiance and me.

M	E
MANNISH	*EX*
MONKEY-FACED	*EXOTIC*
MANILA	*ESTRANGHERO*
MIAMI	*EXILE*

I smell the dead skin of her perfume, Poison by Dior, full of Jasmine—under oath as the first national flower of the Philippines and loving it. She smells like Margarita Moran on her winning day of Miss Universe 1973 and the papaya whitening soap she used twenty four hours before. Sampaguita with bleach and a touch of Vitamin E— ELEGANT, ELONGATE, EARNEST, EUROPEAN. The nationalism flakes on me, dead stars are stars and she still found a way to unfurl past her time. Through me. She's coming onto me. Missus Pia Angelique Diaz's Ballet Philippines starved physique presses onto me from the inside of the beaded corset, our bodies touching across time. I sweat like the smell of the second draft pick, like blooming in summer when the heat sours the sex and all that's left is an orchid's face, defiant in arms with monsoon or heatwave.

I look like summer in winter, a velvet tablespoon of vanilla, which is to say brown but in America, commercialized as a freckled ice cream. Lick it. The ex fiance gropes at my chest and reminds me that they are breasts. I feel Pia stiffen the butterfly sleeves, making sure my shoulders are constricted and mighty. I pull the zipper up and Missus Diaz's spine elongates against the stem of my vertebrae. She whispers something repressed in my ear.

The hair on the back of my neck chicken feathers, fowl. Foul desire is ignited and I quiver, seamed together with Pia and I know somehow the love I killed back home has spotted us licking each others' scents.

My throat becomes red with guilt and the betrayal heats the shades of jade on my ears and jugular vein. There's a heartbreak that's mine, there's a heartbreak that writes me letters forwarding them to addresses unknown. I found my heartbreak exiled in between the waning and running. A heartbreak transplant – Pia and Phillip's purple gowned romance from four months ago, engagement ring on her deathbed, and it finales like this - into a full hybrid propagation, slick even against death bed friction. I surrender into Pia's figure, I am awkward, edging towards a confession not meant for her.

I look like Santa Clara's November Bride, out of season, out of doom. A bride I could never stand to be, not in my homeland, not here. I drape myself in Pia's dead love. Pia the killed, me the killer. Together, I perfect her romance, I'm her perfect revenge. I learn Pia's shape, Pia's dreams, Pia's collection of runner up pageant queen poses. Her toys, her playthings. I am her next, her rebound. Pia's dress presses harder around my thighs, waiting for my buried desires to come out of its tight-lipped cove. I am held, contained in my shame, and I try not to think of Siya who I left— the first and final kiss, Siya's long hair waiting to find a balisong to cut the follicles, to gift to me, under my pillow, Siya's well placed haranista right in the middle of the busy University of Philippines street where everyone could see but no one did; no one saw Siya tuck the orchid behind my ear, near birds excreting, contaminating a lagoon.

I'll remember the nervous jawline that still crooned better than a drunk tito on Undas, my promise to save myself for her, on a wedding bed, then, the excuse of family obligation, the HIV in my ading, the airplane ticket I bought, the luck I never believed in - the remorse bubbles into a petite morte, a tiny death. I am guilty.

I carousel down the stairs to begin the night with Phillip. Pia licks inside the inner lining, hugging at my malnourished thighs. The General awaited me with a handsome sum of fifteen potted orchids in exchange, which was more than the roof over my head salary. I enter the ball. I scan the room full of pinheaded men with jacket pins and every girlfriend, wife, mistresses, comfort woman finds a femme fatale way to turn to me and laugh in a perceived attempt to look like a super model.

A month later the General sent me off with Phillip for a seaside vacation. This time, ten orchids, from Luzon, he says. Where the recruiters found me. Phillip asked me to wear a peignoir set and bullet bra.

So gohn-dah, my beautiful, Philip says, butchering the Tagalog the same way his men pulled apart my home: gold burnt limbs against crucifix hard ons.

The fabric lost its shape from overuse, I realized perhaps I was in another girl's panties on day two. I came back to a vacant house, the General's house. My suitcase that enclosed a medium stack of letters from the love I killed sat wrapped in a single string bowed vertically and horizontally. I read the front of the envelopes who's faces and characters warped with salt, ink and longing.

To: Vivi, mahiwaga ko.
Fr: Sinisinta mo. I'd die without you.

On the top right of each envelope, a postage stamp with sharp perforations framing an orchid and their names refusing latin names: *WALING-WALING, WHITE MARIPOSA, SANGGUMAY, PILIPINAS*, P9, 10 cents, 20 cents, 100P. I ripped the inner lining of my suitcase and place the cards in the inbetween unseen place, promising myself to read them later when Phillip wasn't in the car, when I wasn't on Phillip's porch, in Phillip's living room, in Phillip's mind, in Pia's panties, in Pia's dresses.

In the midnight hour, I prayed that my sleep would walk me to the airport. I had five days before my work visa expired and I missed the love I killed back home. I bought a ticket, I took my suitcase. I'd see what I killed, what I didn't say goodbye to, I'd fly over the sea so I could borrow months that could come.

The next morning I woke up to Phillip, who sat on the edge of the fainting couch I slept on. He handed me a Manila envelope, blank faced on the front. No to, no from. I dug my hand inside which met a paper cut on my left ring finger. Inside American dollars, American forms, and,

Stay? Just a little bit longer? he provokes, exactly like an American Dream.

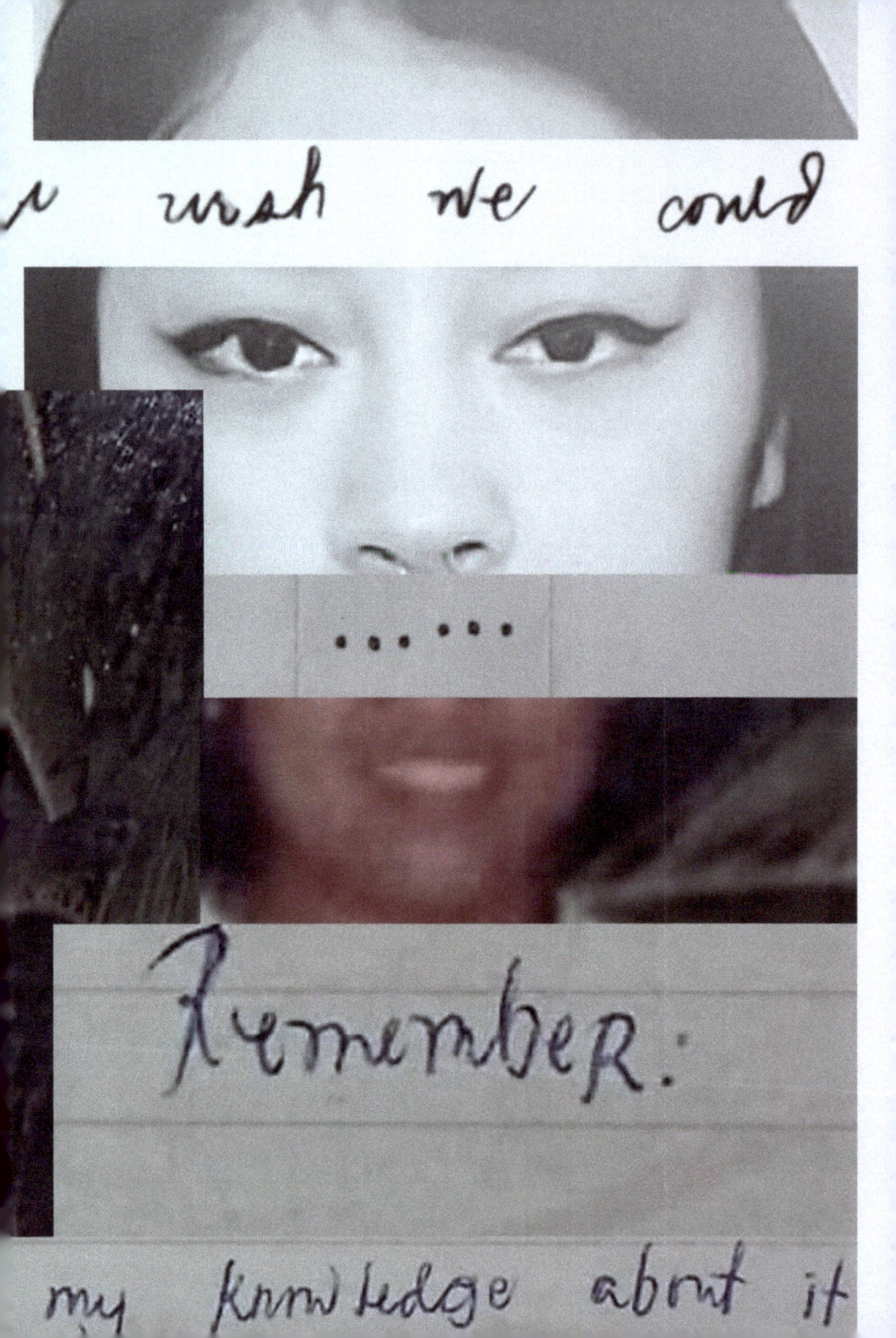
i wish we could
......
Remember:
my knowledge about it

CLOSETED LOVE
WILL CRAWL
OUT THE WOMB
LOOKING
LIKE YOU

the orchid is gay

(i probably shouldn't have told you that.)

she'scourtingsomeone
from four decades ago
she's asking me for my forgiveness
she'scourtingsomeoneandtellsmeishouldcallher

Tita.

she'saskingformypermission
titaasksformyblessing
as if i'm her father, handing her off
downtheaisle   except
she'd never admit to an aisle

she'dratherdie as a   friend.

by the time you've read this,

                          still no
blessing. friendly fire catches friendship
by
    the time

you read this

(what is   out   )
i would've met this Tita,
              greeted her
                    @
(the   outing   )

40

Sea-Tac International Airport.

(cry in   o)

SUSMARIOSEP.

this is (o)

the reunion

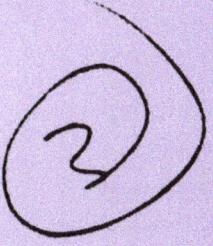

Interview with Queer Descendant 1995 & [From: The Love, Lost. Back Home.] By [To: The Lover, Dormant. Over seas.]

[To]: Thanks for being here.
Queer Descendant 1995: Of course. Well… Are you happy?
[From:]

[To]: Yes, of course. The first time she's in America.
Queer Descendant 1995: Are you in love?
[From:]
[To]: Yes, I am so happy

Queer Descendant 1995: What do you love about each other?
[From]: Makulit! Talk talk talk all the time.
[To:] Her laugh. Her smile.

EXT. towards SilverLake Thai House
          's outdoor
          heat
          errr…

     fire sears
     iron gates around

                    Rico's grin,
     grills.

                    RICO:
                    (commands)
                    every Alviar
               pelvic floor formed to   *Touch it.*
                    nervous,
                                        YES MAAMSIR.

                    VANDA
               eyes laughter
     she jitterbugs towards the protective steel
               holding the humiliation.

                    Rico
               laughs.
                              C'mon c'mon do it.

VANDA

(head to
palm) leaves
no seconds

Why? You do it.

Rico

stays absent
dangles hereness & neverness
straps on love

Vanda

(S-succumbs)
presses
her smile
to the flame.

Letter

Love,
i wish we could be
                    today
&
tomorrow

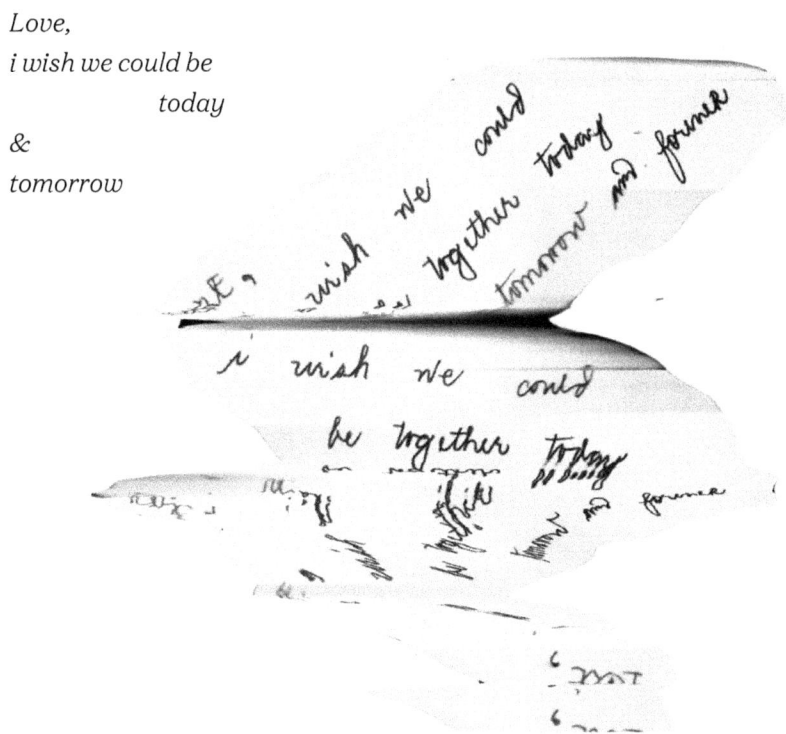

you [n]ever,

forgive meaning to my
    always tomorrow [has gone]
        you're forever
            [not] .

you need
me? i'm wishes to whatever
here to time affection

you
comfort
you.

& since it is a 19th
especially sweet
profound shortcoming

pleasure continue.
i found birth

on the 12th
i miss you
could i steal you in 1990?

should a million Junes best
c . . . . o . . . me.
[back]
. . .there couldn't be a better

                                                        beginning with a

                                                                after that
                                                            the very best
                                it takes to make a   year

everyone takes us
makes to make a very happy year. Health and cheer.
it's always and you always
always too many

just accept this day.

i hold that you're dreams.

ACT 1

@kuyadaverichard sports his marriage on IG

to a filipino woman. she's ilocano
        like my mom.

            points her lips;
             taps with her food slicked finger on a bowl of
             suka, a plate waits with no words and a full mouth of rice
             what's this?

suka, he says.
            the next word he utters means spicy vinegar.
            i don't write it down here because
            i can't remember my knowledge about it;
            not everyone should know my tongue so intimately.
            i'll make you beg for me to annunciate.

even when you do,
        my mother
                is a chicken stretching
                her neck, widening her
                eyes
                in my
                eyes,
                removing the roof
                of my ngiwat
                brick housing molars
                in river gold ahead
                of my tongue.
        shhhhhhhh.

tbh, i crowbarred my tonsils just a few hours ago when
        my lover came into my mouth
together,
        we killed the priest.
        it wasn't even role play
        when the spanish rolled in their graves.

plato, @kuyadaverichard continues in spanish.

his wife chirps like the unknown bird of texas,
she continues to peck pop quizzes.
what's the word for when you eat with your hands?
she shovels a mound of shame spun sadism, spicy vinegar, rice and bistcc,
chews it down. he repeats the question back in tagalog. then in ilocano

here is this man, speaking ilocano. praised for his fluency.
here i am speaking english more fluently than jake.

i want to pin his tongue to a dart board and invite all my friends with good aim.
i'll find all the overseas maids and pay them their freedom rate. together, we'll get
elbow deep into his mouth, scrubbing the taste buds off with "brightening" soap.
we'll burn what language he learned to help him remember english is his only
language. make it whiter than he already is. this man who has relocated his
beloved "tagalog-ilocano speaking american" wife to texas.

a white man gets to be a kuya gets to be speaking ilocano on any land. he has
50,000 likes for eating rice three times a day. wowweee talaga! nakakatuwa
talaga kayo, laughing emoji. heart eyes heart eyes in the comments. i am
floating in a bifurcated dimension of reels. in a purgatory of 30 second time
wastes, i see him in his before/after glow up. before he married her, after he
married her. before he married her, after he married her.

before:
he picks up kid's toys,
his hands, hinging
at gun sling waist line,
hurting his back.

after:
he picks up the blanket, the blue
teddy bear,
with his penguin toes.

look at that dexterity!

    he even knows filipino superstitions i don't know.

before:
@kuyadaverichard chokes on a
dilapidated burger,
chokes on his english words.

after:
@kuyadaverichard chokes then
regurgitates ilocano, *bwenas! who is
thinking of me right now?
he counts on his fingers, isa, dalawa,
tatlo, apat. pour.... ah, bay, say, day.
letter d. sino siya d? ehhhh ni dudong!*
the cinema moves on, centering his
wife, outdoing his ilocano, switching
to tagalog as a way to flex.
she plays the bit even harder, *no!
baka man, D-, for DARLING.* public
humiliation fondles his insecure
power, if only he didn't like it so much.

i take a magnifier to my lips→ then his lip to my →lola's lips next to→
my lolo's beside my nanay's and ← back again. i am shocked to find his
face appear ilocano because he's speaking my mother's language. he's
speaking MY throat cut, guttural stop ruler slap wrist. i try to destroy
him again by placing him on my tongue. i raise the back of my tongue to
the roof of my mouth and ejecting fast to make room for the smash of
air that needs to stay trapped to create the *nga* sound. nga nga nuh nuh

nahhhh! i fail hard enough i try something else.
i become the colonizer now, the white man turned husband turned dad,
the spanish crusade, i'm a priest, asking him,
do you believe in spirits!
do you dream?
do you swear that you don't see ghosts or believe in superstitions?
do you have premonitions?

i continue the codex like a visa application mano y mano. he shakes his
head with the eyes of a christian which is to say ignorant ease. no tawny
muscle of resistance in sight.

after 20 minutes of watching him show off his fluency i'm watching his
nose change and his eyes get cat-eyed. was his eyes blue? they're brown,
beautiful even. i try to think them as over ripe bananas instead.

  i look again and he looks like my
father who likes his women exotic and indio.
father doesn't speak ilocano,
  i think.
doesn't use instagram,
  i think.
his eyes are handsome in that loving overseas women-younger-than-me
kinda way.
  i doom.
  i scroll.
  ThereHeIs on instagram
  in a world with my mother in texas. she is so proud of him.
  he makes her laugh in ilocano.

  i've never seen my mother
laughing in her own language, in love.
  she wouldn't have wanted that.

ACT II

play airport music
on top of fave local muscian
plucks strings, with tattoos
no babies cry this time
cept your mama
cicadas clap together
all wings smacking still
ask director sibling
what the theme song
biopic tracks for officer granted
automated sliding door, is,
unblinking eye dry eye
waiting waiting sound,
everyone here waiting thru
so many coming outs

on the potential of misgendering
a 40-year courtship

Rico fits the suit i never got to buy for her. her smize is even faraway. less
performative and caring. what i mean is i want to call her nanay. mother.
tita. like the mother that mothers my mother to mother me. gay mommy
who teaches a closeted gay mommy to love her even gayer children. new
mommy who tells us the truth of our biological mommy.

one mother and a dad
i begged for. or mom. moms? two geis
embrace before me.
in the middle of sea
tac airport. after waiting for 3 hours.
after crying at every other love fest reunion.

in attendance:
        the ones who mattered,
overlooked:
        all of us driving in, flying in from out of state.
materials:
    (1)   hand drawn mickey mouse paper greeting procured from
           stranger asking
    (2)   *who's coming?*
         (1) pen and a paper.

everyone there to celebrate, to love out
loud to love wins! live laugh kodak moment
hallmark disturb.
then finally!...

a narra wood armoire exits
the long line of immigration,

back ache, he didn't find out Vanda was
exported til too late. Rico dodges
my mother. the cameras. sends back the greetings. the whole ordeal.

rice water mixed with the last visitation, the last you know what. a peck flies from Vanda's lips after she runs up

like a young child hoping to be scooped the way it should've been, but tatay was in japan, in a final money made

a sea of strangers watch.
we, also strangers, hearts
clutched like pearls, as if
Celine Dion was Jack, kissing
Rose in titanic, as if
is *this harana about us?*

55

perhaps i blinked and missed it. perhaps Rico, cancerian shell
shocked that Vanda initiated anything at all.
perhaps this love is not for us to love.

the sky lights in the airport should be called grief traps. wet rain
putters with a lead rejection on kilig, on paruparo wings—where do the
butterflies rest when weather forecasts a touch down without touch?

still, all of us windchime, squeal shout, riot blur parade blur like it's
Pride 1969. we ruckus with our esophagus riling up behind our kn95
masks. my mother hushes us, removes her eyes. two wilted buds
enclosed around her 19 year old hopes. i wish i knew what
those hopes were.

what desires keep her unmoving?
what illusions promise her silhouettes the real deal.

a light bulb glimmers behind her ojos, sturdy brown
benguet pine cones—where a *maybe* sets heavy on her recollection
of stolen moments. i mean stolen as never

taken between each other—martial law taking
them in, saying *kiss now*, display untouched insiders
for Duterte's army man. i wasn't there but maybe the kiss landed before
the baton did;
i wasn't there

the need to humiliate PRESENT!
then masturbate OVER & OUT
there—at least they didn't die—

her iris pops;
for the rest of this visitation,
i'll never see her replace it. we stand next

to her, all glow
in the dark filaments. twisting
like bulbs, placing our hands over
already lit

sparklers.
how dare we become a fanfare, a welcome basket, a carnivale.

Rico,

i want to talk to the people who saw you kiss in the middle of the night in 1984. record shows no one. record shows that we are both astrologically cancers. record shows we have both loved people way older than us. robbed cradles. are stolen children. you who smells always of the sampaguita that calls you over WhatsApp.

i want to believe that love can change us. i know it does. but when you take Vanda's hands to hold, as friends—as kaibigan—as my tita's-sister's-batchmate, Vanda is unchanged, steadily ashamed, the way you like her.

always,

AN ACT
DECLARING THE WALING-WALING ORCHIDS AS THE SECOND
NATIONAL FLOWER OF THE PHILIPPINES IN ADDITION TO SAMPAGUITA

EXPLANATORY NOTE:

the people know, you were first. you were okay not being the only.
you are best as a highly lucrative business. highly disfavored you are
enchanting.

ENCHANTING — sold out, trafficked, over cropped.

it is increasingly rare to find you in your natural habitat.
you are never home! when can we go back?

DECLARING — SEE: denouncing

DENOUNCING — self effacement, accepting lesser importance and
significance as the country's second representative flower. SEE:
assimilation, equal

EQUAL — you are important as long as you declare yourself second. you
are treated in
ADDITION — after thought, to the sampaguita.

ACT — in this ACT you will hear the sampaguita's declarer again, the
senator omits WHO declared the orchid the SECOND.

ASSIMILATION — you have a knack for adapting, being anywhere,
flexible.

but where, if you had to choose, where would you like to be?

ALONE — *this is fine.*

Approved,

i am happy.

ACT III

delivered in stoic ivy
brutalist buildings love
Vanda. the exile.
every genus found
you. every gender
appropriately
on display,
in my pores.
on my nose.
searching rabbit
stitches together.
to love
a love thing,

and pangit alabaster.
the me that's you,
the second silence.
a will, a way to fetishize
fumbles you. we are
mistouched.
Vanda. they're looking
blackheads jaw drop
they pat down,
holes. sinew
pulls looks
deflates fetishism.
a prized possession.

living pro
of of an
is
land
con
quered.

FLATTERY, AGE (TWENTY) THREE

        young enough to stay
wantin' to impress
      her, with her hands
full of weedy bouquets, me,
       mouthful with my own lovers who
pass the test,
       charioting her to SeaFood City.
 afternoon full
of trap door lullabies
       biko stickin'.

she knows so many more
       confusions, *she's so smart,*
even angels get starstruck
      by umbilical cord biases,
i'm gonna be smart like her.

angel baby go on, bark
      now, song and dance rounds
spiral town sing any namesake
      of the 40s and 60s coo
the retirement home mama who
       serves ending dream meals at:

                you gimme fever / when you kiss me
            fever when you hold me tight / FEVER! /
               i'm your misses / and daddy won't
                       you treat me right.

i entertain the wrinkles of time
       sitting next to other hairless elders
abandoning grins only to eat jello, unpeppered
       meats, family goes bland, applauds
 a baby monkey
in a mini red dress, crooning every third Sunday afternoon til the clock
strikes pre-teen.

the evening breeze caressed the trees tenderly
/ but you and I came stumbling by /
got lost in a sigh were we

       my face plasters inay under her breast,
newspapers of penny stacked success,
       mama labrasones through the death stink
halls of Providence Mt. St. Vincent.

Earth angel?
Earth angel?
Will you be mine?

in public i've shut down
       the precious postures
for better off, coquettish demands.
       the difference of lottery and poverty
side steps escape —perhaps because i was born
       with hips that queer rocked any thrum
and rolled without morning sickness.

suppose a chimney of a man,
mixes up the names of every Vanda, p.s.
count your own birth in that.
despite being the referee in any
and all outbursts — babies aren't birds in nests
birds aren't butterflies migrating
aren't nine year old angels
who need lessons on how to
survive a drenched night, to *see what it's like!*

sans sibling
who i did not take with me,
for which a guillotine has already dropped
in place of the front entry
this way, a piece of me

nikki is alive—
without the fun of treasure
hunts or caterpillars hidden inside tupperwares with blades
of longing, behind a display of stuffies,
to be found dead later by Vanda—
sleeping in disowned bed space.

would you have ever thought we would
learn to pathologize babies
        in therapy. then,
take a sip of hot water
        and ginger honey.
i hope we all burn our tongues.

for a woman who says so much -
        filling the air with lemons, flower spikes, fried
        bangus, her the duty, the honor, a militia of pride, glory to the
        erasure, genuflecting to the opportunity of labor, a house
        dress competing with the skin,

        tell them we live in a house,
two floors,
        we are happy white
fence, picket line
        roses, latchkey walking
        chandeliers, seam ripped over and over again
— she doesn't say much of anything.

i babble words of nothing.

FERTILIZATION

I- i'm not pregnant, yet
i'm gestating a suspect
of hide-n-seek
presence of fifteen organs
in my shiny depression—
O labellum, O belly—
the unseed sticks, arranges
into five whorls. printed:

there's a lot   *there.*

                    today,
my friend tells me, semen stays
            stuck   inside   me.
there's a lot   *there.*   completely changing my own dna.
there's   *a lot*   *there.*
eggs who might stick a middle fingers up, are also,
still, changed by this secretion.

        & what about all the dna that might shape a face
        i forgot? & what about the fingertips of you, who trace
waves a tut, who walks a runway outside the notion of xx
capabilities & what about the descendents trying to
bury themselves on this page?

V- sinta's dna breeds last
laugh giggles & braids our faces.
scientists falter at our stubborn existence.
mountain top surgeries,
never perplexed, we
doesn't care, we loop
hole, we, sneakily tenacious, &
in ur face

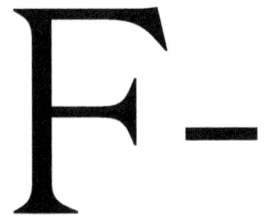**F-** never have i ever found the metaphor for never having ever thumbed a catalogue of donors, a price tag on a bag of ball sack vials of semen —this falsehood of the only future wayfind. instead~

mid-sentence strikes and there, in the pore of this period . is the flatnose eye is the cheek of the long eyelash sepals at the edge of the paper is the thumb that may bleed from fondling the book's wish, only to find the seed right in front of you, now, eye-to-eye scanning between the pound of corazón and the fetal curl of this comma , an alive screech against your arm, birth babys you, finger hooks the relikaryo hoop ring pierced and pulls the mallungay-starved-marrow out the page break.

~village~dream city~child, this too long linger dons something fraught and poetically broiled something like "the moon is a swallower, never a spitter, never wasteful" but instead i feel an imminent violation and dare to appease, to call it fair holy. maybe that's the only thing that might make me honorable to the fertilized catholics in my family.

O child not mine, you are of each of us, anyway.

H- HOLLOW

here's a picture of a bird of paradise. their children are lavender. they look like Duwamish clouds, stubborn against an insistent sun. an ingenue awe, uuwuuu reminding, *here's some gray in a sundrenched place. this picture reminds me of* inay,

the louisiana sun punctures every pore, all
that's left is expired salt.

why do you stay in places so cool?
is your fascia stuck in the jets?

i wish you had that last kiss,
never again. my veins countdown   days, for your woman
with no reason. the sampaguita   is flippant, making the
moon shut down,   it's feigned
          romance.

muted.

i haven't seen the orchids yet.

the night begins at 1 am,

and so does the day.

IDK.

mama, my duster is so saturated in peach i see double. i am matching
the turquoise house on the corner, smacking my tongue like tsinelas,
sitting limegreen on a porch swing. the rock is painted blue. the gate
is metal and spares the flush of your face. my trying to remember is
perpetuating my forgetting.

*

my mother and i forget a lot between us, before us, and what's after.

we both say I DON'T KNOW the same way she performs the sign of the cross. right before we sputter the truth.

nay, what happened to   *mom? did you*   *meet*   *? no,*
I DON'T KNOW she was   *. sick? with what? EWAN.*
lola was young. EWAN. she died when   *.*

my mother calls her mother (*my mother*) in english, and)*your lola*(in tagalog. my lola is someone we know but do not share.

i call my mother nay, short for inay. she calls her mother nay. my pinsan call our lola nay. but i am told to call her lola. when i try to talk about lola aida, i say nay. my grandmother is my mother, accidentally. i wish it was on purpose. my mother is my grandmother. my mother's mother is on a patio with a bird of paradise, closing the blinds from the outside.

i am searching for
i am searching
        search
        & ~~rescue~~

...Take this as a simple kupcake to be remembered from moment to moment...

a
world
slaps me across
the   face.
my mother's palm lines
tell on me
and
i'm a new sun.
we are both   cockfighting towards

each other.
cuckoo
i wonder if   each generation
splits   the   distance.

i wonder if
the   imposter boi
spitballing towards   me
will be born

w/o
silence

ACT IV

don't run your mouth

      i am what my orchid feared:
another mother abandoning her.

      i am what my mother wished:
running away to paradise.

      i am what my mother dreamed:
a orchid as distant as her first love

      i am what my mother hoped:
something she could never know.

the head appears 180 degrees from
where it will finally bloom. take your
head and turn it a full 360 degrees,

that's what it's like to
grow through secrets
and become the truth.

traits

my titties are maroon, pointed, in attention - in attack. a lover who overwatered me once said, *your nipples are like my mothers.* it's a weird comment, especially since the comment takes off my underwear, my clothes, my secrets rebelling on my mothers forbidding. some secrets are obvious.

i assume i am not like their mother when my nipple rings bleed through a subway in nyc. did you know it's legal to be bare chested in the streets of new york city? i don't expose myself, inay wouldn't want me to be tender so publicly. this ex lover tries to find their brown mothers in my features— i wonder if their mother had the three long strands of black hair at the bottom of the nipple or if they're just counting that the areolas get puffy when they're disappointed, and mean when they're aroused, or better yet, ashamed.

i become that on stage: mean and aroused. i wring my torso into an hour glass, counting shame. the sand drops in a stream. time is land, piling on top of itself until it is deserted and buried.

time is so soft, i get statuesque, grinding every former lover's mother into pearls. i wear them on my neck, taunt them to choke me. they almost, but don't. like my mother, they lay still, holding hurricanes.

kai means ocean and orchids grow there too.

their fingers lilt like a plane in turbulence across my crocodile belly. i am limestone guarded and naked. my pussy holds secrets too. pop culture loves a tight lipped bpussy, something that contracts but never expands. they wisp at my edge and a volcanic slumber wakes up, unwoven. my mount pubis is not flat. kai jokes and says, *it's for all the pistil you can take — it's ancestral.* i know how to erupt for hours n hours n hours n days n years n weekends n miliseconds n minutes n *anong oras?*

i am worried that i'll become ravenous, emptied, hard, protruding, whole. myself. i cannot stop if we start. can a volcano stop if it is slammed between two tectonic plates?

\fuck/no\

on skin contact, i make spikes, one of them 3 inches, i hide it by wearing the high slit dress, i ruin it by way of menarche, there are spikes in all directions, too many nodes to track. i succeed at erection but only kai knows that, it only happens when the spiral has spiral'd. i succeed at sequence, fibonacci flat lines.

my dysphoria is versatile, it goes yoko star. the horror of pleasure inserts, folds paper cranes into me. i laugh and ask, *what does it feel like?*

their smile erupts and he says the word i hate most,
home.

gender markers

ill orchids bloom everything around them, besides themself. even the weather blooms foreign clouds, the stars hang like drool, painting the sky with its own shadow. the drool levitates in still air. in a room where repression found struck clay, purple earth and called it the only way to grow.

the orchid resists its curvature- even though the garden is chirping. strange things happen. breasts swell off chests that didn't know they could do that.

naturally,
everyone shames their predecessors.

biologically,
orchids flex autonomy,
has spare expressions right in its pockets
saving most for the midnight temperature drops
in fact,
plays with it,
does it all.

nature offers choices,
tries one on you and
wonders *is this alright?*

even nature gets it wrong sometimes.

PEST CONTROL PROMISES

never take a photo. scrub the internet
of any evidence. no crumbs, no snail trails. every onlooker beaded,
stringed into a seashell chandelier. build a charm, assem-
ble in Internal Family Systems away from origins.

i.
dry the piña into fibers — dye with favorited pick me not.

ii.
place beach sand in a woven bag.
walk the length of your gut.
spill
hibiscus oil, hot enough to magenta.
give empty to sinisinsiya's uncle who
tried to marry you,
carry to the cliff, where he will
fall
and
maybe?
even

—————

iii.

snuff the coal ragged of my burnt hair. by the way, i shaved it. buzzed
the entire lineage from my follicles. when midday strikes, after lola's
disapproval between lolo's explicit deer boy hind leg, keeping the back
door open, inviting us, me and you, to stay together– i'll walk knee deep
in the flash flood of rice terrace fondling. 28 years later the flood lines
will fishnet the stretch marks.

iv.

apo widens to you. complete with circumcised treasure. don't forget
about me, spells out the the trash, the shit the pesticide pillow talking
your Walgreens hair dye. oh we will cry plastic crystals when you return
into your non-binary grandchild's ovary, your gay gene grand-girl's
brattitude tone, this is where we will learn that the man)the myth(the
dyke (the legend) you learned to love for liberation requires your weeks
old, lying yes.

three hundred thirty six deep throated moons later

not all hips are ship wrecked. but mine are learning what to do
with the wet of surviving typhoons. shake shake shake. flesh
off the coral spine. shake off the stories drummed
in my cochlea, not mine. every night i'll hum a throaty overtone,
and i'll start the day at 5:12AM after the murmuring leg spread and again
at 3:43PM after bump bump bumpin into an ancestor that shows me
how to use my hamstrings to straddle bounce budots beats properly.

today i wake up with new sensations, ones that not even the stamen
of blood drain have felt. i wake up with old rivers dried; new rivers prayed for;
the bundok that stays gyrating. i wake up with BOBO possibilities,
BOGO eyelashes. twenty eight pounds of weight that exits
thru a baby island. a cyst
archipelago rumors true, self centered
shimmer best with chismoso, take the twinkle
of the evil eye, even bakunawa jealous
chatters.

we are all centuries in the clay
kiln making. kulintang bells will fuse to my
wrists; ankles. just like so; so descendants can hear me. there is;
no other paths to be explored except; this one that you read me on:
sound out the bell toll, shovel the nilaga over and over and yo-yo me
back to the loop on your ring finger.

now tell me, is that real?

I wanted to make another dance,

but this

is the only way I can move right now

i choreograph new islands

st. malo dances me in circles til i smash
or pass? on shrimp skellies til meat ejects
ejaculates on my feet
stomp, jump, fah-lap, step-hop, abandoning
a sinking ship : nuestra señora de buena esperanza.
swearing tsinelas smack mga antennae, eyeball,
and thready hair legs . mosquitos shrimp
buzz into angels
tell on me:
my blood is sweet as a fugitive
calamansi rind, thumbed.

how to : be of
extraction does not mean we have to choose it.
just because
iknowyouknowweknow how to survive crossroads
of crisis does not mean we have to accept that as our only life.
just because
they can clap off
beat rhythms doesn't mean i won't imagine
a sleep where i can sleep.

peep the brain grooves, valleys
ROLLING! in action right now . CUT! it
is threatening. here are our backs, carrying
wings, arms like moths like cicada like love

bugs. our faces
purging . salt
crystals form under
milk ducts . we will
cry this new world we will
bark like a dog . chase.

they'll never find us
on the map . below sea level.
the ocean gulps mud . fresh water
queers have never lived here.

except us and a frequenting man
who pretends to be disgusted.
he will choose to betrothe ugly money first,
so don't worry, we're safe here with centipedes, legging
us on, unlike crocodiles who maybe cry
more than an alligators myth of TMJ,
SNAP!
eating at the center of the marsh
THRASH.
until they claw up our stilted lake view home,

looking for us, undercovers.

doing what we do.

i walk with the baddest witches towards the End of the World

for ylva, kiki and moonbear

i fly
with banana
leaf wings.
paint the town
in the coolest
beaux bleu

;

a peaches hymn
on sun drunk.
we are so sober *we are altered.*

;

the river is polluted
with plantation factory forgetfulness.
the river is dirty. do
not swim in
nasty.

is some water
more sacred than others?
some say this water
is un alive

New Orleans
softens the ground with opulent shrines.
here, a lemon baked in *transsexual fucking, duration: 24 hours.*
here, River, a bundle of grapes will split their heads open on
the dehydrated boulder all for you. rapid fire are the oranges,

all falling farther n farther away. i hold eleven stems of budded orchids
i survived enough to say, *here, take this me right now.*
i aim them to top eachother.

river bruised
i pray that red white and blue
come back to the refracted light.
WARNING: the flags.

i bless every ancestor who
couldn't have the joy of queer sex to go
on then,

get freaky.

remedy: move to cool place. hold water for few weeks, no long-er. withhold. water; other-wise risk. SEE: DISEASE. do not force feed.   do not force water. SEE: WATER. keep in darkness. SEE: PSUEDO-BULB. migrate at night.

ACT V

four months after saying it

Rico and Vanda paraded in plain sight, i slept in a humid Louisiana may. in my sleep, my left and right leg dangle on each side of a saltwater crocodile. speeding down a swamp i've never been to. this gulf'd edge is as close to the islands i know only by capsized memory. humidity makes my face plump. dewy with plant sweat - plants that are so rare. rare like extinct. someone will call it an [*you say it*]

i'm surfing a swamp, afraid. afraid and rushing. looking for my [*say it for me*]. the water is threatening the earth. the earth slips into it's mud. i feel her in the air. taunting care. right there is a small island. the small island is the back of three crocodiles. i don't see their heads.

there's a swarm of something that's supposed to be beautiful. a migration of wings. they're cloaking my future. i can't see. there in the swampy archipelago is a mother crocodile, my mother crocodile. eyes of a disfavoured [*say it with me*] because it replicates this reptilian mermaid. she bears her head, a shut jaw.

i jump towards her. afraid to be eaten. [*please say it*] mouth never opens [*for me*]. my eye never blinks, they well up until they give up into tears. i'm a butterfly, but not really. my proboscis unfurls and sips on the minerals. sips on the tears.

90

EPIPHYTE

the lands beauty is stolen, copied and sold. Vanda, is it terrible
my body copied
your beauty
your land? have i
stole from you?

orchids rarely get to date anymore. private property and real estate
tycoons cleared out our resting places. there's a stranded stem, quiet
with E- EXOTIFICATION, an empty privilege. i stand in other flower
fields now. unsettled and wrong-planted.

i trust myself to rot my own assimilated histories.

my own trial is in not gentrifying myself. i promise unforced entry of my
spirit, it's uneasy when your head hangs upside down high above trees,
roots suspended, different than *stay here, don't leave.*

It's a common mistake to regard [O] as parasites.

mama, call me a slut again. enough to fill the grief of your stolen jewelry box: filagree filipine gold, sacred heirlooms, rosaries, saint diwata, witch doctor mirror, diniguang, pray over the coconut oil.

SLUT[123456] — i dedicate this next jack in pandora's box, to you.

[1] bees pollinate and are never hypersexualized

[2] they fuckin' like bunnies! (bunnies multiply in humps, are not desexualized)

[3] fruit bats teach two manananggal how to hang off a branch using the thick of long hair while the other flips upside wrapped face up against the waist, to hold eachother in the peach's pit of an inner cheek, suspended in a breeze, sway.

[4] against the breeze, leopard slugs who spiral spit in each other's indigo organs, spilling out the side of their necks, heads atop blue sky, licking concentric circles, gripping breasts into chest, swinging mucus rope taut. taunt. drop.

[5] even a tree trunk cruises to be pressed up against

[6] stays open

TERRESTRIAL

today, i perform outrage even though it might kill me to eat another moment
of despair. we bust an alien-face-earthly-existence & don't run.
we-us-i-me-you,
    bloom inappropriately.
      bloom without tradition.
        bloom to be a madonna but not so madonna that the holy water is
      finger fucked by every person that walks in.

when did it become the nature of things for babies to be foraged?
                  N-neglected.

it's the nature of flowers to be foraged.
even just to adorn your lover's ears.
it has always been enough to be plucked willingly.

ingat.

i used to be a perfection
of circumstances.

a roof over our head
food on the table there is no
dictatorship

frying the money
on the wok, fired

up n leaves during this Seattle freeze.

are we not grateful?

washing clothes in the dirty river.
we do not lug home to hang
on a line.

section 8 2 bedroom,
atleast i wake up
lux eye crust
to mop the floor,
teach my younger sibling to pee
& shit in a toilet.

here in america
you do half as much.

here we forget

to teka muna
like a daily chore.

grief is a luxury.
$2.99 $5.99
top shelf

buy only what you need:
light, food, house, retirement plan.

i buy what i need.
i need a lot.
my needs are extracurricular
mental health activities
see-saw break-it-downs.

orchhidacae facade
inay wilts.

kid,
you could try to
separate fiction from
Last Unicorn fantasy and
defame yourself. all that
matters is

mommy orchid survived.
you can tell because
she stifles herself from blooming.

dahil sayaw

this dance is what my bad dreams
look like — the uneasiness in the bilboed lip,
the attitude of romance finding dread. i
dance as if aerial roots, brittled— like the
Nature Path granola bars that are swept up
resourcefully from Providence Mt. Saint
Vincent's Retirement Home Dining room. all
this to be lip locked, lock jawed in my every
generation shoulders. the roots defy wrap,
they rot because they like me are shoved
into a soil medium that makes no sense, but
they teach a $1 bill how to be hypermobile.
bark chips, foam, cardboard, "seattle."
"portland." "manila." "los angeles." orchids are
cosmopolitan. orchids are big city, city big.

i dance so loud. i dance because saying something without
sayingsomethingisalmostlikehaving
somanywordsanddoingnothingwith
them.howmanycavernsofsilence
couldappearbeforeyoucanmakeout
theword?theimage?evencaveshold
echos.idon'tknowhowtosayitin
thislanguage,idon'tneedtoknowmy
mothertonguetoknowwhattosay
because i shouldn't be telling you anything to begin with.

i will begin like my mother. I DON'T KNOW. I DON'T
remember. I DON'T KNOW. i am so bloated these
days. i push my tummy out to imagine where i
sat in my mother's womb, high or low, boy or
girl, all or none. I DON'T remember that i am 28,
the age of my mother when she had me. i bloat
and wonder what i wasn't allowed to birth that
keeps me flaring my ribs, tilting my pelvis,
stretching my abdomen.

some days i feel so wide with silences that are inherited.

why did you leave her?

i don't remember, she says.

humid air fills the place underneath my bellybutton, it's a bit like a plate
shattering but more like winter — a season my body learned. my ovaries
love that unison 5! 6! 7! 8! releasing at the same time, threatening twins.
threatening double headed truth. i know my threats like i know my
promises. clear and

order CUT ALONG DOTTED LINES

m a i l   o r d e r   f o r m

CUT ALONG DOTTED LINES

SEND TO:
Orchid

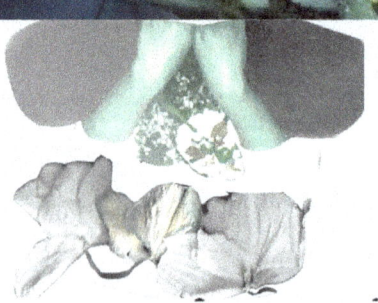

in the months to come.

CUT ALONG DOTTED LINES

just because
orchids can defiantly grow under any circumstance,
does not mean the mothers are not sick.

suppose there are two

way, a rebel, hi
i wonder who is "us" ,

who could sew a wedding gown for the whole town to wear

she ran a
kiddo, i made   *trouble*

could it be   b   e,   never was   be, is it
every island   who asked what   what
what barangay.

,

i wonder,   her   ,
guise of duty

versions of the story.

her   truer truth

where's you husband?

the bride she never was was never documented to be,
every tita who asked

maker,

don't you miss us?
her wrist her face, her controlling

sige ngarud

inay asked her dead father for forgiveness over zoom.
lolo died, secretly of covid
tito sent a picture of him
dead over fb messenger.

     snaps flicks
of going going gone.
deceased. mama repeats
    audacity, archiving
only when time foams at the mouth.

       falters
at a mother in climax. how is this
     i think. i thought the catholic
more glass sacred, more reserved stained, more
knee bled genuflection
when death comes wrong.
i backhand forgiveness.

catholicism does not run in our veins, barbaric things do.

         did he ever receive the vaccine?
           inay ignores my questions.
         say defeat kept *100* rejected
           offerings on the altar.
      days before a final moon river
           urged to see him
              isem.

pixels sorrow harder.
zoom condolences
preyed. recall
our last dance.
the first time my beauty mattered.
my fingers, brown vanilla
bean pods, stemmed

like lolo. my lolo and i
are very pinakapogi
together, i can end

queer as in sex bomb

MOTHER MACHETES AN EGGPLANT / TO MAKE TORTANG
TALONG / S/HE SPLITS / IT IN HALF / DOUSES / TALONG IN THE
YELLOW SEA / OF FROTHY EGG / WATCH IT COOK THE COLOR /
OF HER BROWN / WITH A SICK GREEN / I AM RADIATING
VIOLET / PURPLE WATCHING AND LISTENING / IN BETWEEN HER
BITES / *DON'T ASK FOR MONEY, MY DAD, TATAY, ANAK DO NOT
TELL ANYONE* / SHE SPEAKS / A CLOAKED TONGUE / AS IF THE
REST OF US / BUT ESPECIALLY / HER / WOULD BE ASSASSINATED.

i met my mother's chicken
once, in the house's coop she used
to work in. in the home that my lolo didn't die in.
the chicken was beheaded. my mother's head there instead.

clucking ~~un~~likely fears.

there was no funeral,
no travel back home no
death ritual. and if there was i
wouldn't know, my family doesn't know how to
contact me. to them i am NO. 841, which is embarrassing and hopeful.

*ORCHID TIP
#JUNE301995*
Orchids thrive
best topped
by eggshells.

easy, at a window or under artificial light.

inay lives alone. the first time kai met her she flirted
with them. which is really libra of her. my guess is more than me,
my future lover would be her caretaker — a spouse she could never
imagine for herself.

my mother's only tactic around security is to flirt and deny. exactly like
 a rose garden, which we aren't. one time my therapist said that i
probably don't know i'm flirting. i was horrified. *babies flirt as survival*
she said. great, i'm a baby floozy, favorite flirt flitter, dimple face packer
under miniskirt, hips with venus divets [press your thumbs there] great.

my mother flirts her way through life. flutters her eyelashes. cracks
jokes, eggs, hearts. she's so funny, it's irritating.

but when security comes knocking on her door looking tall, dark and
successful she locks the door, anchors her bird-necked umbrella 45
degree angled from the kitchen wall at the top to the top the front
door, places her two plastic dressers and a piece of cardboard under
the door, where light shows through.

when security comes with a man bribing me with $20 telling me to just
smile i take it.

i

need

groceries.

IN THE DREAM I CARRIED YOU

[insert image telling her i love her]

keiki faces genesis

There once was a Vanda whose waist was wrapped by a strange keiki. This keiki shoved their way out of Vanda's fisted mouth, as if Mt. Apo's rock side could crust over her face. Keiki, stubborn, erupt, foothilled across Vanda as a heavy headed bud, everfused to Vanda in a piggy back ride. Keiki is old enough to be almost too heavy for such things, but Vanda has carried her weight in suitcases for a decade now and this is nothing. Vanda has a tendency to shuck the baby's laugh off her back, a weight of river water sloshing in a shared bed instead. She doesn't like to be touched so often.

Keiki is in its third bloom: two half faces, one stem, and a shy set of toes painted pink. Vanda severs keiki's fifth name for luck. Gel short for Angel. Gel scales an armor of leathery leaves across Vanda's bladed back. Leaves grow out to be thick and emerald and shining - extraterrestrial wings on a terrestrial woman, Vanda, who is far, far away from the tropic of pearls and orange fanta in plastic baggie for jeepney journeys to gallivant to Manila Metropolis with 10PM curfews or else a smatter of batchmates will tell on her or else sacrifice of safety or else a first kiss taken.

(Who else could be) kakawate voice engkanto chanting:
heaven is us alive, especially in a time like this.

During this time, another orchid in Vanda's stomach shoves their uncooked breath towards Angel's hooked foot, latched against the xiphoid process. This twin's anger stirs in contemplation of hard launching, has double horned sepals, hoofs, and a knack for being undetectable. They gestate a year behind because Angel gambled with the pacific rim and *we won!* flipped Mt. Apo into Mt. Tahoma and placed it against Vanda's cervix; told those tiny roots in Vanda's tinier stomach to stay sleeping, maybe even to never come out, even threatened, like most mantis do:

If you absolutely must exodus from our shared sunken atlantis, our mother island barely floating, far, I'll eat your heart still, take your belly into mine, take your queer bend into my left hip socket, and your eardrum to only beat in the night, only then can you come along.

Angel strained to utter this, but the roots shake best at the edge, and we must never ever ignore the roots. Yes, they may have thrummed the spirit line to incoming keiki, but there was no answer. No answer is still an answer. This answer cleaved the tail and all its bones between the two keiki.

Any time Vanda's tummy streaked the severed queer in their stomach, Angel would speak in the quiet, and if you could hear anything at all it would sound like:

soonsoonsoonsoonsoonsoonsoonsoonsoonsoonsoonsoonsoonsoonsoon

After all, there is something wrong in the apartment off of Ambaum Boulevard and Angel needs to find out why the ceiling is made out of popcorn, silver spack and why Vanda's hair is wiry and erect. Zero buoyancy.

Some say orchid flesh only burns when a horticulturist triple the height of Vanda, and six times height of Angel, enters. His eyes never still, they wiggle left and right very fast. He comes from lost love, his eyes say he born too soon, his heart left in a hospital incubator, never retrieved. The eyes never stay the same color. They bounce between gray, blue, murky green, and all of that together is the baby shit brown he'll never clean up. Just like his eyes, his voice can quickly wiggle to a sudden boom, the kind that make the estuary diwata take their tadpoles underneath murky rocks and wait it out. Angel doesn't believe in waiting. Unlike the deer caught in head fracture, they leap, they distract. They play with Vanda by jumping on her back and begin poking the cumulus of tobacco smoke. Twin keiki looked through Vanda's belly button and stole the air, the nicotine gambling away serendipity. The two keiki pounded the eardrum, the seismic eruptions and recorded it down for the madrecacao tree who can read the difference between life or death.

Kasi babae could not find her way back to her sinta,
Kasi the love is misplaced onto a promise of a man
Pero the man finds himself on a mountain

Would you not want him lost atop, around, in, out your skin forest, the place you know so well? Would you not want to keep his skull on the bolo knife as an apology, an ask for forgiveness from your sinta?

There is no secrecy in magmatic laughter. The moment counts down and spills out of Angel who takes all three of its orchid faces and shuts their eyes tight; follows the love that forms the future sibling - their roots fuse to stretch as far as they can to the original exile, Vanda home-gone, running.

Angel can not sense the way back, not even an aso ear can pick up the coordinates, as if there was no echo to locate. Angel skips years, turns kingfisher and coos to Siya, coos to sinisinta, hoohoos to kai to ocean black salt sea grime, grows up and turns diwata too fast. It takes at least seven gestations of orchid hybridization to even consider such an ascendance, all to build a compass in a place with sunless light.

Vanda inhales souring testosterone, wishful estrogen, slurps the tremoring river diwata in her throat, who turn into the vom-green of an amphibious construction sign – is the body turned to soil, pressed up against a wall with the orchid whose three blossoms are future fingers / holding our face stitched from our first stomach fish flop / joy pressed into pulp / Vanda, whose spine / in Angel's chest / who turns / into an experiment/ ~~of red, white and blue~~.

a secret goes BLOOM! inside a B- burial jar.

i am sure she sang to her

Vanda sings as if singing was grieving her own cultural suicide, which is not entirely true because she's homebound on a silver karaoke set. *Go anak! I need to pee.* Vanda passes the mic to Angel who takes on the chorus like the pig that bled out for the family celebratory lechon for their one-time-never-to-return homecoming. Angel sang back to 1999, like an orchid song bird who romances the head of a lechon pig, the pig head was carried by the lean arms of a Lolo who didn't die in his home, but did wake up Angel from a nap with all the porky frankness of death. Death could be so normal it could be funny. The laughter would bellow like the crackle of basted skin, roasted over and over in front of the family unit.

When angels sing, poverty lifts, milk prices drop, all people are fed, get to go home, the oceans are free, ships with baby formula and flour land on the shore, and healthcare is just a bus stop away with the purchase of medicine amounting to ten dollars max. Vanda sees an escape out and lands on that future a few hemispheres off. When a song bird finishes a song, the voice will jewelry box lock back into the fingers twirling addicted to tobacco smoke. The only applause is the karaoke machine that cheers back in a 1990s synthesized brass. 100! 100! 100! cheers the digitized screen. *We won!*

Vanda ran back from the bathroom, as if the stream of her piss finally foamed and flushed the loneliness, the orchid is singing, a lasting intimacy, a keepsake, a way out.

We won in a victory that belts and wanders to the embarrassed country side, a victory that dis-eases the very fact that the motherbody could cum first. Do orchids think of the diwatas as another nailed god, or just another being that will grow up as a departure? The notion wilts orchid, til the only thing butterfly about the diwata is a balisong wing.

If only Vanda remembered she is an Orchid, Angel would have never outgrown her.

PRUNING—Dead head the family. Take your fingers and squeeze them from the stem. Use clean scissors or a knife to cut the waist length hair. Grip the hair like a throat. Each strand is at a death march. Cut them free. Return to the stubborn ones in a moment. Cut everything down to an inch. Follow the stems to the tree arms. It's Emilia Almazan. She's so quiet you can barely see her crown shy with the sky.

extremities

lola aida warned:
never marry a nuclear weapon.

==orchid's don't need to come
with warning labels.==

but, they do

have the tendency of being susceptible
to burning from excessive exposure;

in extreme cases
this may result in their death.

There couldn't be a

try   after that

It takes one to know one

No one told me
      ading was coming.   other,
         rebel says,

      Not listening   I warned   Nikki

sly,   birth certificate   knew
they   born blue.

      oxygen pushes out their lungs easy-lipped. Asthma.
           smoke inside, never opening a window, always
    a box of camel wides,   appeared   orange tipped filters
every 48 hours.

    Flicked the ashes– the butts–
     house with   silver
    karaoke machine,

our ends expedited the killing,
           soft.

Face Bust

i caught an o   sexting. o   's don't use their phones
well. O asks me to teach her how to open the app again. the
app is open. the words are in o   -cano. for the first time
in my life i didn't let my face bust...

nay, you close it like this. i perform the millennial dance of
swiping my finger across her phone. magic.

i already knew what to do. i tucked my lips into my mouth
until they were gone, until the memory found home in my
inner cheeks, until my own face, just-a-mouthful titties,
boi-g?rl-bakla pussy betrays. wins.

Nikki I need to tell you something.
We're at a bus stop waiting for the 128
from SeaTac to Tukwila.
It's about mom.

Okay?

I think she's a Lesbian.

Hahaha—

(1) Laugh like a barricade, a
standoff

(9) Laugh like a talk show host who
has a live audience of martial law
officers

(7) Laugh as if it could bring every
enforced disappearance back

(2) If you feel like crying, cackle
never again, never again.

—that's a good one.

I pause.
It is, isn't it?

the philippines is the second catholic nation in the world. divorce
is illegal and so is gay marriage. when i think of my mother in her
dormancy, i think of the love she'll never get to know on her land.

the car ride from the airport was quiet. the atmosphere asphyxiated in
dollar store silk flower. Rico and mommy orchid are muttering to each
other. mommy orchid is like a middle school girl, smiling and insecure.

*//DON'T ASK HER ANY HARD QUESTIONS, DON'T GIVE HER A HARD
TIME BECAUSE SHE HAD A LONG TRAVEL//*

there was only an 11 minute drive from the airport to the section 8
apartment she escaped to during the peak of my fathers domestic
violence. within that 11 mins Rico asks my mother "where do you want
to be buried. here or home?"

mommy orchid swiftly replies, "here in america."

ading asks why. why not back in the philippines. i think my mother
knows that america is a delusion in itself. (or maybe, what if, the love she
killed back home, was never real?) i think it's safe for her to breed more
delusion. (which delusion is scarier?)

i think she thinks she's free.

today, I saw mama

hold hands with Rico

up a trail in Topanga.

I wonder if

they ever held hands in Bangar, La Union.

stigma

remember   neck was covered
hickies?

   blistered   , daggered,
like an oyster   ill from   .
    stigma. like a runaway
maintaining   granddaughter who
glorified   blood stealing leeches
thought   not even
kink

17 is too young to pull off something so slick.
   choose   bruise   to a ballet
class.

    lengthen my neck, trying   depict a
poor orphan in a kings court, dancing
    supper. those king's think
       gorgeous
          poverty.

i got chicken legs.   manok
      a swan. you couldn't cook a swan
into adobo nuh uh.   chicken tendencies
cannot resist the urge to   cock
       means   i open my
mouth, i'll crack the dawn   call all the

souls home. especially the ones awake
fucking mothers who want nothing more
than their mothers.

Mothers   are
terrifying.
        i want   that   terror.

        make sure   no one could eat
    me.   they'd try
    me ad nauseum.   they realized
    inedible.

        stigma   split down the middle of my
            .

    voyeurs dig their   in me, i'll tell myself
    it's because i let them.   throw me to
    the wind   til i spilled the sticky wax of

    jealousy is the fertilizer   this soil
        thick   legacy of envy   cuz we
    bloomed when they were threatened not to.

    17 is young enough to think i could over
    power our shared abuser.   free
    enough to flashback

WALING WALING
are not wallflowers

especially orchids like Angel who come from places like Vanda

dormancy is all around me.

There is a frozen sound between Vanda and Rico. In an LA winter, the seventy degree weather wrings out near my ading. The carbon breath shared by everyone in the Silverlake Blvd apartment is kept there. Not even the seventeen dogs that walk past the building can sniff out that there is an absence. Now you're in on the secret too.

MOTHERBABY's lover-not-lover scatters through the air and lands on walls like the chromatic glory of a disco ball. As long as that disco ball doesn't spin, no ignited light would get caught. Keep the disco ball in pieces. Those pieces cotton mouth before becoming a skittles taste the rainbow campaign. The remaining saliva checks in at Burbank Airport and makes sure the barangay of Facebook batchmates knows, Rico is here.

I am the age MOTHERBABY had me. I am the age Siya contemplated taking her life because she never got to see mommy orchid emerge, just what came after. I wonder what happens when you resume love without seeing any of the ugly attachment issue blow ups, or what of the mutual afterglow of questionably toxic make up sex, or the years of watching some hopes fade and being there for depressive episodes, what bickers cause a monsoon, what birthday rituals, favorite cake flavors or sweet friends would be shared? What jealousies? How would they have gone about loving each other living a block a way? A barangay, two jeepney rides? Would they have jumped in the river, and who is the better cook? What experiences did they miss on each other? We blow helium into the questions and tie them off with party ribbons, 99 luftballoons.

I can't shake my first private moment with Rico. We were at my mother's run-a-way lottery won apartment that she's lasted in since 2005. 15 minutes from knowing her, Rico pulls out three boxes of polvoron:

Ube, Original and Variety, a gift from the airport. My mom is impressed, waiting for me to perform the greatest gratitude that's ever existed. I tell my body to go WOWEE TALAGA for me? Bubble bubble docile cis-energy bubble bubble.

After my immigrant-eldest-daughter-performance-rituals close, Nikki pulls out a small vending machine toy from LA, for my mother. It's probably a magnet. My mom has a refrigerator full of tourist magnets, places she's never been, places she'll never go.

What is dthat? A sex toy?! Hahahehe. Rico tries to get me to laugh along. As if I am not my mother's daughter, but my mother's friend, another pretty thing, another option to flirt with. A very OUT! party rebel girl at a discotheque in Manila in the late 70s. 80s. ABBA is bumping. PYT! Pretty Young Thing plays next. Rico sees my mom like her mom, like her family, half-accepting, conservative and impossible.

Ew. Ew. Ew. Okay maybe this is fine?? ALONE—this is fine I am a sex positive human. 15 minutes ago Rico could just be an abrasive queer community member. Is Rico gaymom? My friend? A stranger? A dad? What does she want with me?

After several hours of indifference, I snatched Rico's ⬜⬜⬜⬜ at me. I wish I hadn't. I wish I had pinched each of her eyelashes off her eyelids. I wish I would've told Vanda about the look and how it looked just like the man she got the citizenship and a couple of kids from. I wish my spouse didn't notice. Then of course, because we are here for dessert, the cherry of gender silent bubbles. Rico figures it out, finds out a nonsecret: transexuality. her brain grooves do the E=MC^2 meme at the legibility of brown boyz2men masculinity, masculinity she'll keep at bay, an expansive masculinity she denies herself. The love I thought INAYBATA had carmelizes and because the kitchen burner is still on,

it ruins the bottom of the bacon greased pan. Rico's gender is being
a bachelor who takes a liking to my mom's consistent denouncing of
her own unlabeled desires, unlabeled attraction. Rico's gender likes
to turn Vanda's out. Rico's gender counts on failing that quest. *(I
CHANGE MY MIND. That's not gender its [PLEASE, you say it.])*

It is Christmas Day which doesn't mean anything in our family except Rico
is here and Siya is nowhere to be felt, so suddenly we are in holiday spirit.
Rico looks like she's melting on the couch. Probably because my mom
got her up to walk to the airport, to arrive three hours before departure.
MOTHERBABY refuses to get an Airbnb even though I offered to pay for it.
Nikki appeases and thinks it would just be easier if they hosted the two
reunited love birds in their open floor plan apartment. I am scared. I am
protective. I have already bloomed. I do not know how to shove my orchid
face back into my orchid node back into my orchid cunt and fold into
my big orchid energy. I watch as my siblings' final hope of our mother
changing under the spell of love fails.

Rico took an edible. MOTHERBABY asked my sibling to take them
to church in the same breath they asked to go to a dispensary.
MOTHERBABY hates weed, but if you're masc, then it's fine to hit the
bowl. Puff puff. *You know that has weed in it? Is that alright?* Says
Nikki. Rico replies by not saying anything. Not saying anything means
nothing is on record. Rico ignores the question three times. Pass.

INAYBATA cries when Rico doesn't wake up for Christmas Dinner, a special adobo made by my sibling and I. Special ingredient: mania in dedication to our mother's queer coming out, for her acceptance, for our acceptance.

I have a god complex I didn't ask for. I am in this position of seeing everything. Omnipresence is a son of a bitch. I am trying not to run but also what's wrong with running? What's holier than fleeing, than being the ▓▓▓▓ sheep? The scapegoat.

kai chariots me away from the whole ordeal, there are things I am going to leave out now, especially the part where MOTHERBABY cries, the coming days of days of on-again-off-again, what are we? It's got to be fake news that Rico is high as a kite on the couch, like oh shit, is Rico a fuckboi? The Stoner TomBoyfriend™? kai lays me to rest in the small grove of orange and lemon trees in Montecito Heights. I need to recover from the funeral I just walked into, this double generation saturn return love fest.

In a family of queers, I am still living in two different worlds. Rico would likely never amount to much, she is the originator of my mom's obsession with vacant love. This is not the queer redemptive love story my friends want to hear.

This is not the love story I want to write.

OFFICIALLY: MAMA'S-SISTER'S-BATCHMATE

I sent mommy orchid the music video for Blue and Orange by Kimmortal. It's based on a real life experience of Filipina lesbian couple, Darla and Cecilia. I don't know if Rico and Vanda would identify as a real life lesbian couple. I rarely ever hear them utter gay. They're not even facebook official.

The music video is like an alternative universe where Rico and Vanda melt into blue indigo true actual tears and orangey fungus of sunsets unshared. Complimentary colors. They say goodbye together, again. They're each others one and onlies.

But this isn't THAT music video, even though the tsinelas fit: based on a real life couple, that couple is also filipina, that couple is long distance...

When asked what their relationship agreements are, mom replies standing on a mound of pan de sal breadcrumbs and mixes instant coffee for Rico. The music video we're actually in would be filmed by the Pope. The Pope would open up on an image of two crocodiles, eating two hearts. The final scene would be a feast of those very crocodiles, if we can scale back their green leather skin, cook them like lechon, the heart of mom and her lover apple between their teeth.

"Rico is like you all," mother says in another attempt to (m)other herself from the pot of soil she's already rooted into.

I WILL NEVER FORGIVE THESE UNNATURAL SYSTEMS

for stealing away any mother's possibility to know queer love.

I WILL NEVER FORGIVE THESE UNNATURAL SYSTEMS

for stealing my own possibility to see mommies in queer love.

I WILL NEVER FORGIVE THESE UNNATURAL SYSTEMS

for stealing.

```
              ENTER
            [erosion]
   ...i am her first living example...
         ...i am her truest,,,
            queer love.
```

we wanted the skim. we filet'd the top of our arms until they're ginger. almost nothing. we have less time to taste so we want bold. don't be shy. give it to me. less is more, they say. we pack a punch. it's easy, with our petals already clenched. perpetually in bud. unbloomed. we are pretty weeds. usually this grasp is empty. faces are facing into themselves. i couldn't tell if this was a nose or a hamstring. dramatique, sinister with unwavering insistence. *different, they're special. unflinching, they'll clench onto your heart.* the clench does not cut. just a pinch. a skinned wrath. razercut disruption.

we wish you could remember what compassion is when you're not using it to protect

you.

you're holding an orchid in your palms. this book is made of orchids. lucky you, you are holding the ass of the orchid, go ahead smack it, you can. i know you want the back of the book, in your right palm. your open left palm messes up the orchid facade. fine, it has an undelicate spine. but don't tell anyone that. this story is in your hands. choke it by slowly lifting your palm to the side lobes, avoid the avoidance. you are the tree in which i root on. you are the pot in which i get shoved into. so, hold me, please. hold me.

they forgot to spill the coins into the concrete. this is what happens when you forget to fight for eachother. but maybe a chicken. a white feathered freak. or maybe a

lola shows off her property. first, the iron gate, next to the highway. the house is light teal. she is the elder of the barangay. there is a man on a scooter that says Kumusta po kayo. lola is telling him i do not know my tongue. he is jarred when i open my mouth. it's stuck in a pot. lola shows me tatay's ashes. he's stuck in an urn. lola shows me the same bench i took a picture on when i was four.it hasn't moved for 25 years. the outdoor picnic area is where they take naps in the afternoon when it is too hot. she has a garden. she has many plants. no orchids. her hair frizzes out. she's been sleeping a lot. all her children are so far. i tell her it's good she has been resting.

someone tried to tell me my lola is touched. touched in the head. as in a little bit crazy. z-zany. as in deranged. her catholicism is not spiritual, it is a symptom of being touched. she never talks to me about catholicism. she talks to me about if i have kids. she asks me when i am coming home. she'll dm me a paranoid catholic propaganda a couple hours later. it's a chain message. it's not her.

gay side by side a gayer grandchild, both cleaved at the neck, will.

DIWA'TEH SAVE US!

US!

DIWA

DIWA'TEH

ATE 'TEH

SAVE US!

DIWATA

EH

(Step 1)

- - - - - - RIP — THIS — PAGE — AT-THE - DOTTED - LINE - - - - -
                                |
     PERFORATE — YOUR LAUGHTER— | TURN AWE CLOCKWISE -
YOUR PAPER SHOULD UNFOLD— | _ _ _ _ _ _ _ _ _ _ _ _
                                          - TOWARDS YOU—

~ ~
(Step 2) LEAVE A MESSAGE AFTER THE TONE

place the phone receiver to the sky,
run towards the lover on the other line
when you get there, call yourself back.

(Step 3)   keepsake

     hold your mother as conductor
----------   --------------- -   --------- ----------
          on your   vocal cords   --------------------
------------------------------   ------   ------ record keep
                                                the
                                     screams---------------
     like this-------- ------ ---------------- ------- —
----
     carve a line for the intonation ------ - on your
                                                favorite vinyl
----
                    ----
                                                     keep
     sake
     ------------------ ------------------   ---- -------
     -
                    --------------------------------------- . play
------------- -- at your wedding

*Extremely
showy*

**Long
lasting**

I'VE PROBABLY BEEN ON YOUR WINDOWSILL

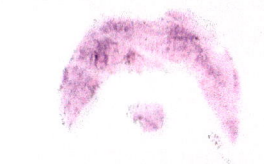

OR IN YOUR MOUTH

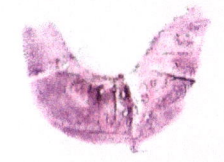

BABYMOTHER:	MOTHERBABY:
I'm not going to tell her.	
	You don't have to
She's not going to accept you.	
	I don't expect her to

lola opens the gate from the inside. INAYBATA is on the outside, as a surprise. MOTHERBABY is atop the gate, INAYBATA doesn't know. MOTHERBABY spills roots over broken glass security, all the forked iron. BABYMOTHER enters, tries to lock the iron gate. MOTHERBABY's faces multiply by eight then five then six. INAYBATA doesn't notice MOTHERBABY's thirty blossoms. INAYBATA doesn't know MOTHERBABY is an orchid straddling the inside outside of her childhood home. BABYMOTHER comments on the flowers to lola. lola recognizes the flower. she's been growing MOTHERBABY. even on the otherside of the gate. she tells BABYMOTHER about MOTHERBABY. how MOTHERBABY grows to five feet. that MOTHERBABY came down from the tree. emila almazan died of orchid sickness. she died before she could be hunted down.

MOTHERBABY is five feet of reward
thirty two inches away
from knowing the bounty of
baby mother mother baby

Did you mean:

WAILING

last sacrament escaped
flesh mortification, escaped
sacred union, escaped
st. diwata lives in between the
waling- sepals slip -waling,
waling- the lips bite- waling,
waling- petals brown thick -waling

apex against gravity
even if you are the smallest
flowering cluster
excessive pain will
be locally known
provincial princess pageant
almost winner

St. Therese is
WAILING
WAILING
WAILING
WAILING
WAILING
WAILING
WAILING
WAILING
WAILING
WAILING
WAILING

WAILING
WAILING
WAILING
WAILING
WAILING
WAILING
WALING   WAILING
WALING   WAILING
WALING   WAILING
WALING   WAILING
WALING   WAILING
WALING
WALING
WALING
WALING
WALING
WALING

St. Diwata is   WALING
WALING
WALING
WALING
WALING
WALING
WALING
WALING
WALING

WALING

Ignore all

Always correct   "WAILING"

namesake the orchid and the mother will stay pure

Vanda is adorned by saint therese's lessons in ever-fucking orgasm.
born in 1515 saint therese joined a covenant of incarnation. therese is
the first in defiance resisting double standards. an orchid is an orchid,
and a name is a series of trials and terrors.

therese has a connection with god so earthly she cums in the hands
of a woman who longs for a gender unrecognized, a manliness and
godliness. effeminate.

each finger,
          a tongue
 iron tipped
disappearing.
 plunging
          vein smatter
 alive between
          two thighs
just those two.
she who pulls out
everything that gets
          in the way of loving
          a butch, her a masc,
          him?
this single sweetness
is too hard.

too bare.

waling in Saturn Pisces

I wish she would love who I love.

MOTHERBABY is 29 years old when orchids are not enough.

MOTHERBABY survives more years. plucks the ghost from BABYMOTHER's roots, solves the secret BABYMOTHER knew in between ejections: only one of them is an orchid. MOTHERBABY falls off the bone. never have they ever had fifteen doctors appointments in three months. never needles, but always a horticulturist extracts injects the pages with another hormone, always a reply kicking flesh, bruises that make the belly spotted. similar to the one donned by mothers, single, issuing restraining orders. you know the one. BABYMOTHER goes with. watches new life, places ash, uglies the forehead, perhaps no more hypersexualization.

two nations, against abortion, abort her, MOTHERBABY is left eating her own puso out. cries like she shoulda in 1994. cries into absent minded hope carried forth by lengua against lengua tastebuds against fear of leaving each other like that in which BABYMOTHER did. cries without eyeducts, those utang na loob tears. the water will be kept for the water birth, water baby, water page. water the page.

there's a thirty three eyed Diwata living in INAYBABY's house, INAYBABAYLAN's loca mind. broken cupboards are replaced with purple rose narra wood. There's a banaba tree Diwata who licks everyday humidity and expunges out everyway they've done the dictators deed for them, for free. the killings stop, and, we stop courting our own homicides.

One day Diwata is caught in love. this DEATH, will be placed inside a chest cavity, *can we borrow yours?* Diwata sprawls mid-air inside of mid-lung. you will be recruited to check the cupboards for MOTHERBABY, who likes to hide, who becomes a starfall when she does her surprise acts to her own INAYBABY. MOTHERBABYBABYMOTHER asks the author: *Take me with your future.*

keiki babaylan

sweet and unsick, two granddiwata
hip hang. alive. hypermobile atop
a swollen anak. loves love enough
retraces airplane pathways over Vanda missteps
F   A   L   L   B   A   C   K!
in love. grows a garden. she bouquets misgendered
dances, feeds pancit to a hundred person room,
gays go wow, Vanda wears her 1989
smile, squeals, *they love me.*

granddiwata skip up to 1966 Vanda.
          to 1995, four days early of July.
    keiki orchids run faster than the spacex rocket ships whose
debris litter the Philippine Sea,
     the Tongva waistline.
     & Baguio magellan-killer struts
            new spits up faster
            than Vanda's face flush when Rico friend
          requested her on Facebook. these twins arrive
      to Vanda and call her

                  inay. ask her things in a language spoken
                  behind discreet hotel bookings, between
                  SUPRISEEE! family gatherings, twenty
                  hour flight, eight hour togethers, call a
                  grabe cab the morning after, send them
                  home, with only the hibiscus onlooking,

the orchids look away, out of performative
mano po respect. lay on her hardy complex.
lay on her winding quiet. lay on the gravestones
of government made pining, catholic staking
of chest vacated. Vanda softens in a way that
no lover has ever been able to accomplish.
F   A   L   L   S
B   A   C K! in minefields. staring at the
pools of human flesh, who grew from places
Vanda birthed. who grew from me.

approximate the conditions

i stay inside lola
        's house longer

than anyone else
        remembers. some say

i'm a little touched
        in the ulo.

        mirror, mirror,
broke the wall.

lola aida, dries
        up. resents
a spat

desire   threatens
        to come back.
i'm telling you
        to visit her
 twice.

already know grandchildren
        tomorrow visits me
at the cock fight,
ring finger gone.

mga apo
      plump cackle,
inherit a silk line of ghosted

phantom
      phenomena are
we, are
      tayo.

I collect orchids
and grow mothers
and none of them are ever
you

Live! At the Arboretum!

we flood the floor with roots, in case of a typhoon. we lock the gates with every word i wasn't able to learn in time. i climb onto the ceiling and grow upside down. hung from a skylight. no one else can enter without first considering what it would mean to touch the consent.

what it would mean for ph, the acid of sweat to wreak havoc — means to have a home you can never rest in. what it means when the typhoon will drown us anyways. it means when the bombs rattled a lola's ear drum. what it means when a lolo's ashes spill over at forced entry. when you don't say tabi tabi po. when you say tabi tabi po and the land is uprooted anyway. one day all the land will be flipped upside down. when the pot is hatched. when the land can't grow orchids anymore because the mother forget because orchid recalls because this day is because

insert ayayatenka here
insert a diagram of descendent dreams here
insert a map of orchid dis-location here
insert a   location

    a map   dreams

in   a   p   o   lo g i e   s

BEYOND
REASONABLE
DOUBT
ORCHIDS
DO
EVENTUALLY
DIE

your diwata grew up to be an aswang, grieves you

when you pass go i won't listen
        to your wishes. instead,
i'll moan into my lover's horizon
        biting their ears full of hope,
declawing every finger of blame
        bending my body, never
covering up again

i'll cover you in vanda luzonica
        remember me?
this lifetime of avoidance
        can shut down
the waiting aswang who
can't keep their hips down
        while you get carried away

To: the night sky full of
shade returned to sender,
diwata wonders like begging,
        could you choose me again?

today i'll burn
        all 88 orchids &
        spread my ashes
at your funeral.

DEATH—
        more alive than i have ever seen

to: past; anak; future; bituin,

                                        since i last saw you,
i have grown wild
ly and withou
t hair.
i have gr
own without ti
me.

i have grown in m
y routine regret.
            i refuse-notice you as a rainforest, sorry
                  i am sorry i forgot the collected
                      harana,
                  i never learned how to sorry before
                      leaving.

                                  i leave with hot
                                      knife,
                              curdling queerness,
                              on my baklaklak

i cut lied
the manok i raised, but

i ate its eggs.
this tropical tantrum
cover up

                         i do not dare you to inherit
                          diabetic, fearful horseplay.
                           i admit, without first
                          impression.

         i stopped the sewage to let you know:
         i sing songs of dayang-dayang, i imagine you-me,

         i imagined
                              days.

      i asked, swirl haired bata, how to distinguish-kiss
                                      a lover.

                            how to tell you,
                         i have, i will, once
                          again, how to tell
                                  how i
                               already
                                 know.

                           i hold hands,
                         no one sees, you

                              play buhay,
                         i pretended i
                         didn't know
                                   so,
                            you do
                               not
                         become of

                               me

but you did,
        against my warnings,
        thank you for not listening

i showed you the holly bush,
        pointed at the red berries and never
        once thought you would know of
                        saging ng puso.

                i did as i burdened
            my endless love denying
                me

                    you
        fearless tom boy prince
            ss, you hoochie
             'd diwata.

              never mist
             aken dictat
           or as a saint.

----
do not fall in love with Duterte.
----

                                    i see
                            you have
                            already
                            forgive
                            n everyone
                            else

i claim,
it is selfish to see
your heart better off.

all i ever wanted

acknowledgments

I anoint my gratitude with an endless
pour of coconut wine, suka, buko milk, a
never-empty rice bowl, and prayers of
exaltation to the pistils, sepals, roots of all
the photo-body, poem-body, dance-body,
flower-body, queer-body of this multiversal
biomythographic book artifact.

Sacred are the lands, across all timelines,
where the spirit of this artifact got to
play, where I was able to grieve with an
unabashed celebration: to Duwamish
& Coast Salish Sea you have raised me,
called me back, time and time again,
salamuchi; to Kalapuya, Chinook and the
lands of the Confederated Tribes of Grand
Ronde thank you for your many veined
rivers and their dream inductions; Tongva,
I promise to never ever suppress my fires
ever again, Altadena, I love you.

To the witch mother, Ylva, my witch
kin: Moon Bear, Opulent Witch, my qt
ancestors, babaylan/brujx ancestors,
Ilocano ancestors, thank you for guiding
me to New Orleans, Louisiana, the many
tongued land, Bulbancha; to St. Malo,
your bayou night songs, alligator cousins,
and lavender lemonades– I promise to
remember. Remember. Remember.

(Forgive me if I have unintentionally mistaken the names of the lands and original people – all these places named, unnamed, recognized and unrecognized have nourished me many times over.)

To the diwata, the pacific rim of volcanoes, the coral sea, the city of pines, and of course, the waling waling orchid, I am grateful for your trust.

I offer my molt to the planet of Saturn in the time of Pisces. Thank you for humbling me with dreams delivered; for teaching me to dream with risque'.

The biggest juicy heart squeeze of citrus suns to my peer friends in Deeper Wider Cohort, facilitated by desire crafter, Corinne Manning– thank you for making this space for me to enter into over and over again; to Callum Angus & the Multiverse crew– thank you for allowing me space to disco ball in spectral spectacle and curiosity! This artifact of waling waling orchids, queer nature freakin' bloomed its first head in *Smoke & Mold*, the first place I was published as 'nawa', as myself.

"Waling-Waling Palpitations," "Licking Each Other's Scents," "When the Exposure Blooms," "Fertilized Deviations," and "Orchids Roll Their Eyes" published in *Smoke & Mold*, Issue 9, Fall 2023.

To the remaining seashells where I ammonite'd in and out of my writing process: M-squad and Leigh, your belief in me stoked my fires during another season of (im)possible times; Mayur, thank (you you you) for all your C.A.R.E; Tin House, Insurreal Life, Portland Institute of Contemporary Art, Corporeal Writing Squad, Roots Wounds Words—I am so glad you foster spaces I could experiment in.

ash good, I pour flames of starry twilight towards you!—thank you for the countless hours of dream tending, advocating, creating and supporting the craft of this book. First Matter Press crew babes, thank you for your letters of awe, for laying your eyes and hearts over and over again, for uplifting me.

Oceans of paruparo wingspan to the mariposa of House of Kilig, your cackles, laughter, ferocious tears always return when kapwa felt lost.

Finally, to my soul-ar system of family, you teach me about love everyday.

kai, you kept me afloat with your tenacious presence on your trans spouse dream bangka.

Nanay, ayayatenka.

NAWA ANGEL A.H., widely known as Moonyeka, is a chimeric creator working across containers of performance, qt nightlife, writing, experimental media and the divine. They're a settler fluttering between their sprawling roots amidst Tongva, Chumash, Chinook, and Duwamish lands. Moonyeka conjures queer erotic joy, animism, Ilocano imagination, and beyond. They center kilig as a compass to imagine thriving worlds for their communities. Moonyeka has the honor of homing into their interdisciplinary instigations as an Artistic Director of House of Kilig.

i was never the siren (2024) is a film re-myth of the Siren archetype; the first installment of their multimedia project 'Harana for the Aswang' realized with House of Kilig collaborators.

nawa draws upon queer and trans performance technologies in their writing, infusing nightlife, icon-myth-legend, drag, and kink. They work across a spectrum of genre: biomythography, hybrid, and the game writing. Recent publications include their multiverse of work centering Waling-Waling Orchids in *smoke and mold*; *am i hot enough to kill?*, an excerpt of (w)horrific hybrid prose, is featured in *The Holy Hour anthology* by Working Girls Press; and *FLASH-BANG* featured in Lilac Peril. They've also been a curated writer for Khôra.

waling-waling palpitations is their debut book.

2025

WALING WALING PALPITATIONS
nawa angel a.h.

THE DYING ROOM
RECIPIENT OF THE PRIMA MATERIA AWARD
annemarie eayrs

BRAVA
violeta garza

FIRST YOU MUST DESTROY THE WORLD
claudia saleeby savage

2024

GREENHOUSE
sophie hall

SUSPENDED IN MY INSECTICIDE JAR
clara mcauley

2023

FLOATING BONES
rae diamond

TEN-CENT FLOWER & OTHER TERRITORIES
charity e. yoro

OUR FAVORITE PEOPLE IN THE ROOM
edited by ash good, lauren paredes & emily moon

2022

BETWEEN THESE BORDERS WANDERS A GOLEM
ahuva s. zaslavsky

EVEN THE AIR, TOO HEAVY
riley danvers

ONE ROW AFTER / BIR SIRA SONRA
sonya wohletz

SOMEONE I CAN HOLD GENTLY
xylophone mykland

STORIES FOR WHEN THE WOLVES ARRIVE
hailey spencer

2021

2020

2019

2018

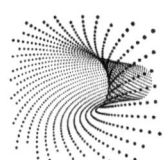

FIRSTMATTERPRESS
Portland, Ore.